FISH AND SEAFOOD BRAAI

MAGDALEEN VAN WYK & PAT BARTON

PHOTOGRAPHY BY COLIN TATHAM

STRUIK

Struik Publishers (Pty) Ltd
(a member of The Struik Publishing Group (Pty) Ltd)
Cornelis Struik House
80 McKenzie Street
Cape Town
8001

Reg. No.: 63/00203/07

First published 1992

© Struik Publishers (Pty) Ltd

All rights reserved. No part of this publication may be reproduced,
stored in a retrieval system or transmitted, in any form or by any
means, electronic, mechanical, photocopying, recording or otherwise,
without the written permission of the copyright owners.

Photographic credits
Thank you to the following for providing props
for the photography: Martha's Vineyard, Claremont;
Boardmans, Claremont; Peter Visser Interiors, Cape Town;
Above All, Newlands; Stuttafords Ltd, Claremont;
Bric-A-Brac-Lane, Claremont; Miltons, Claremont.

Editor: Sandie Vahl
Designer: Petal Palmer
Photographer: Colin Tatham
Food Stylist: Vo Pollard
Illustrator: Marianne Saddington
Hand lettering for headings: Marianne Saddington
Cover designer: Abdul Amien

DTP conversion: BellSet, Cape Town
Reproduction: Fotoplate (Pty) Ltd, Cape Town
Printing and binding: Tien Wah Press (Pte.) Ltd, Singapore

ISBN: 1 86825 225 6

Contents

Introduction 4

Soups & starters 8

Soups 10

Starters 12

Fish & seafood 16

Fish 18

Seafood 26

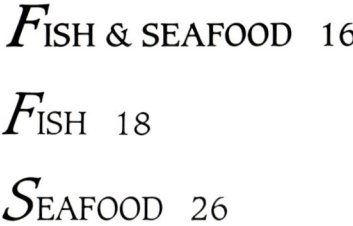

Accompaniments 30

Salads & vegetables 32

Sauces 36

Marinades 38

Butters 40

Breads 41

Desserts 44

Index 48

INTRODUCTION

Select and prepare fish and seafood for braaiing with care to ensure a flavourful, nutritious and easy-to-make meal, or ask your fishmonger for advice.

SOFT-FLESHED SEA FISH

Soft-fleshed fish tend to fall apart on the braai so it is advisable to refrigerate the fish for 1–2 hours beforehand to keep the flesh firm, and they are best braaied either whole and unskinned in a fish basket or filleted, in foil parcels. A kettlebraai, which cooks food on both sides simultaneously (heat is reflected from the closed lid), is ideal for braaiing such fish.

Most soft-fleshed fish require extra moisture — a basting sauce or melted butter — while on the braai. Angelfish and galjoen, however, have a layer of fat under the skin which makes them self-basting in most circumstances. Butterflied angelfish and dishes like Braaied Garlic Angelfish (page 23), need melted butter for basting.

Soft-fleshed fish suitable for braaiing include *angelfish*, *Cape salmon (geelbek)*, *galjoen*, *hake*, *hottentot*, *kabeljou*, *kingklip*, *red roman*, *silverfish*, *skate wings*, *sole* and *steenbras*.

FIRM-FLESHED SEA FISH

Firm-fleshed fish can be braaied whole and butterflied in a hinged grid, filleted and cooked as steaks, or used in kebabs, a paella or risotto. These fish require frequent basting to prevent them from drying out while on the braai.

Those which are suitable for braaiing include *butterfish*, *elf (shad)*, *grunter*, *gurnard*, *harders*, *John Brown*, *John Dory*, *leervis* (young fish only), *maasbanker*, *mackerel*, *musselcracker* (young fish only), *snoek*, *stumpnose*, *swordfish*, *tuna* and *yellowtail*.

FRESH-WATER FISH

Fresh-water fish like *trout* and *salmon trout*, and even the humble *carp*, can all

be braaied. While carp needs pre-soaking in fresh water or a vinegar solution to get rid of the muddy taste, it does make a most superior fish braai. Treat fresh-water fish in the same way as firm-fleshed sea fish.

SEAFOOD

Alikreukel and winkles: Once steamed, they can be combined with other ingredients to form patties which are cooked on a griddle over the coals or in a skottelbraai. Alternatively, serve them steamed with garlic or lemon butter.

Mussels: They can be steamed or smoked over the coals or in a kettlebraai. They can also be added to paella or risotto, stir-fried in a skottelbraai, or threaded onto skewers to make kebabs and then braaied.

Oysters: Normally not considered braai fare, they are delicious steamed in their shells over the coals or in a kettlebraai.

Perlemoen (abalone) steaks: They must be beaten to make them tender. Cook them on the grid or in a skottelbraai, or mince them, make them into patties and cook on a griddle or skottelbraai.

Prawns, shrimps and langoustines: They are delicious braaied, but require frequent basting. They can also be used in paella or risotto, stir-fries and kebabs.

Crayfish: It has a tender, succulent flesh that braais to perfection. Chunks can be added to paella and are great in kebabs.

Calamari: It requires careful cooking, or it becomes tough. If it is to be braaied on its own, first steam it and then braai it briefly over the coals. Calamari can also be used in stir-fries, potjies, paella or risotto.

SEASONAL AND REGIONAL AVAILABILITY

Most fish and seafood are available commercially throughout the year and in most parts of the country. If you want to catch or gather your own, however, official regulations have to be followed. There are, for instance, seasons during which certain fish (like elf and galjoen) and seafood (like crayfish and perlemoen) may be caught.

These regulations also limit the areas where these fish and seafood may be caught, as well as the quantity and size of the catch and the method of catching. If you wish to catch or gather your own seafood, therefore, it would be best to contact the nearest branch of the Department of Sea Fisheries (check the *Yellow Pages*) for detailed, up-to-date information. Different regulations apply for estuaries, parks, coastal lakes and the Natal coast. Information about these may be obtained from the Chief Directorate, Nature and Environmental Conservation, Cape Provincial Administration; the Natal Parks Board; and the National Parks Board (all listed in the *Yellow Pages*).

Mussels and alikreukel may be gathered all year round. Do not collect mussels from areas that may be polluted, as they take in the surrounding sea water and could absorb toxins that it contains and become poisonous. Mussels gathered during a Red Tide are poisonous.

Some fish which inhabit the waters of particular coastal areas — snoek, for example, are caught off the West Coast, and elf (shad) off the Natal coast — may not be readily available in other parts of the country.

SELECTION AND STORAGE

Fish and seafood, whether bought or caught fresh, should be cooked or frozen as soon as possible.

Selecting fresh fish: Look out for clear, bright eyes; clean, red gills; firm flesh that is springy to the touch; and shiny scales which are firmly attached to the body. The fish should also have a fresh, clean smell.

Storing fresh fish: Gutted and scaled fish can be stored in the refrigerator for up to 3 days, or frozen for up to 2 months. Defrost frozen fish slowly in the refrigerator and cook it within 24 hours.

Selecting seafood: Most seafood tastes best cooked within 12 hours of being caught. Crayfish can sometimes be bought freshly caught (still alive) from fishmongers or at the quayside. Select those that are lively and brownish in colour. If you wish to freeze them, first discard the intestine and cook the crayfish. Bought frozen cooked crayfish should be bright red in colour; any that are brown have been frozen before cooking and their flavour will have been spoilt.

Only collect those mussels that are shut. Frozen prawns, shrimps and langoustines should be a reasonable size and should not be broken. Calamari rings or steaks bought fresh-frozen should not look limp or have a white film on them.

Most supermarkets now stock a range of frozen prawns, calamari and marinara mix which are reasonably priced and cut out a lot of the hard work of cleaning and preparation for you.

PREPARATION

Freshly caught fish and seafood — and unprepared bought ones — need thorough cleaning. Gut fish as soon as you obtain them, and remove the intestinal tract of crayfish, prawns, shrimps and langoustines. The neck of freshly caught tuna must be broken immediately or the alimentary juices will destroy the flesh, causing it to fall off the bone within hours.

CLEANING AND TRIMMING FISH

Bleeding: The flavour of certain fish, such as galjoen, is improved if the fish is bled immediately after it has been caught. Cut off the head and hang the fish by the tail to drain off all the blood.

Scaling and Trimming: Slit the fish along its belly with a knife or kitchen scissors and cut off the gills and fins. To remove the scales, hold the fish by the tail under running water and scrape off the scales with the back of a knife, working towards the head. Rinse the fish thoroughly. If the fish is to be skinned later, or braaied whole and unskinned, the scales can be left intact.

Gutting: Scrape the entrails from the slit belly of the fish and rinse well, ensuring that all blood and veins are removed. Fish that are to be frozen must also be gutted, or they will decompose in the freezer.

Skinning and filleting: Leave the skin intact if the fish — especially white fish — is to be braaied whole, as this protects the flesh and prevents it from falling apart. Otherwise, to skin the fish and cut it into fillets, start by slicing along the backbone, from head to tail, with a sharp knife.

Begin at the tail end and cut the flesh away from the bone on one side, then turn the fish over and repeat on the other side.

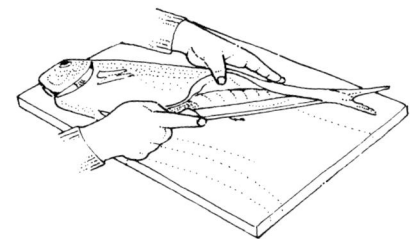

Cut the fillets away from the head and the backbone.

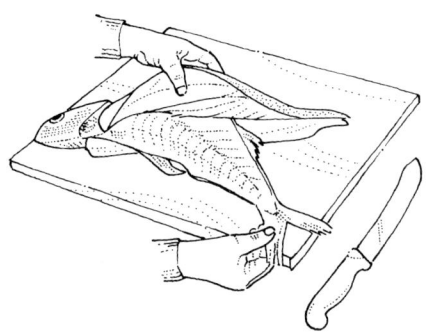

Cut the fillets in half. To skin them, insert a knife between the skin and flesh at the tail end and grip the skin firmly. Hold the skin down with the knife and cut the flesh from the skin, moving towards the head.

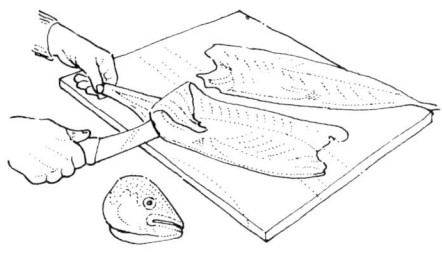

Butterflying (vlekking): This method of preparation involves cutting the fish open, along either the belly or the backbone, and folding out the flesh to form two halves attached in the middle.

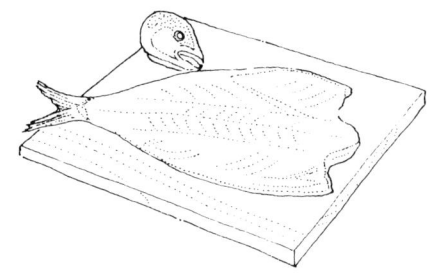

The fish can then be wind-dried or salted and hung outside by the tail for 2–3 hours to toughen the skin. Rinse off the salt before braaiing. Fish is easier to handle when prepared this way, and the skin is deliciously crisp. Elf, galjoen, harders, maasbanker, mackerel, snoek, yellowtail (all but the smallest fish) can be butterflied.

CLEANING SEAFOOD

Prawns and langoustines: These are generally bought frozen. Thaw completely in the refrigerator, then cut through the shell along the back and pull out the intestinal tract. The shell should be left in place, as it protects the succulent flesh and prevents it from drying out.

Crayfish: It is best to drown freshly caught crayfish in a bucket of cold, fresh water before preparing it for the braai. Hot water will cause the tail to curl up stiffly, which makes the crayfish impossible to handle. Leave the crayfish in the cold water for 15 minutes, then place it on its back with tail outstretched, on a board. Cut along the length of the soft under-shell, using a knife or pair of kitchen scissors. To butterfly a crayfish, leave the last segment of the tail uncut, and fold back the cut halves of the shell. Scrape out the intestinal tract and stomach and rinse the crayfish under running water. Pat dry.

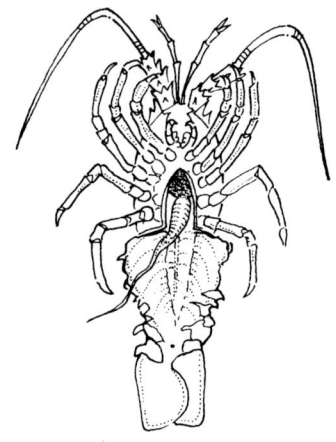

Perlemoen: Remove the perlemoen from the shell by inserting a sharp knife in the lip opposite the row of small holes and prising the flesh out. Scrub the perlemoen well with a pot scourer to remove the greenish film from the flat surface.

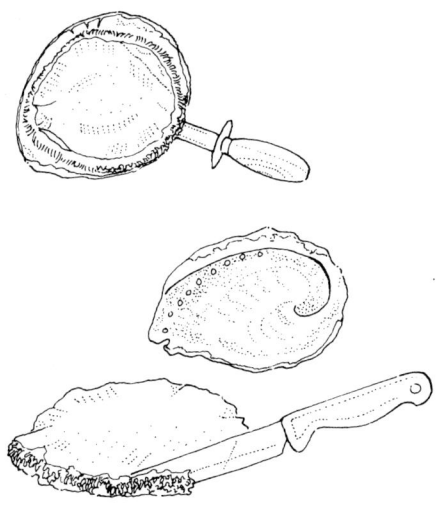

Trim off the frilly edge and the dark area where the intestinal tract is situated. Cut the flesh horizontally into thin slices. Beat them with a mallet to tenderize them, or mince them.

Mussels: Mussels should be cooked as soon as possible after gathering. Do not keep them for longer than 24 hours and ensure that they are still alive before cooking them (see below). Leave them in fresh water, preferably in the refrigerator, for at least 1 hour, to allow them to empty the sand from their systems. If any mussels remain open, discard them. Change the water several times.

To test that each mussel is still alive, tap the shell firmly. If it does not close immediately, discard it. If the mussel does close, pull off the beard of hair-like growth and scrub the shell until clean.

Oysters: Scrub the shells and prise them open, using an oyster knife or other strong knife. Serve in half shells.

Alikreukels and winkles: These must be steamed in the coals before being cleaned. Place them, open end up, in moderate coals and let them cook in their own juices for 30 minutes. Remove the 'trapdoor' at the mouth of each alikreukel or winkle with a knife and prise the flesh from the shell. Cut away the dark stomach and slice the remaining flesh thinly, or mince it.

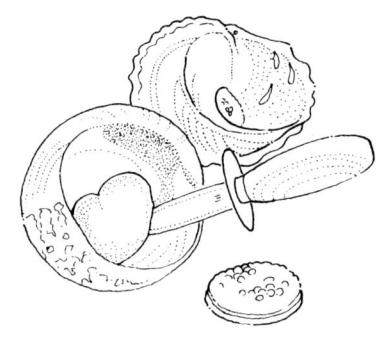

Calamari: To prepare a freshly-caught calamari (squid), grasp the head and tail sections firmly and pull them apart.

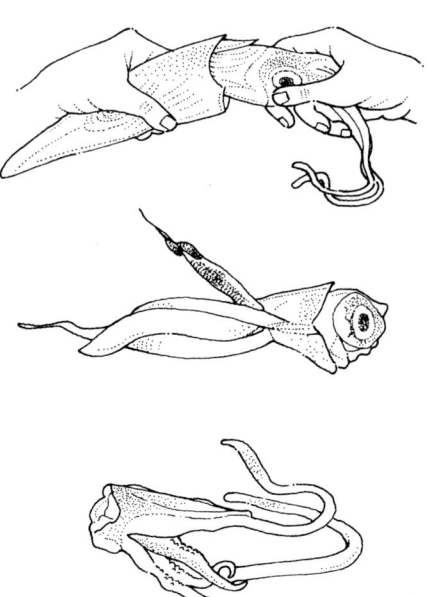

Lift out the ink sac and discard it. Cut the tentacles away just below the eyes. Discard the entrails and eyes.

Remove the small round cartilage from the base of the tentacles and pull out and discard the transparent tail skeleton.

Pull the fins away from the tail cone and remove the fine, outer membrane from the fins, tail cone and tentacles.

Wash the flesh thoroughly and dry well before cooking. When using bought calamari cones, ensure that the tail skeleton has been removed.

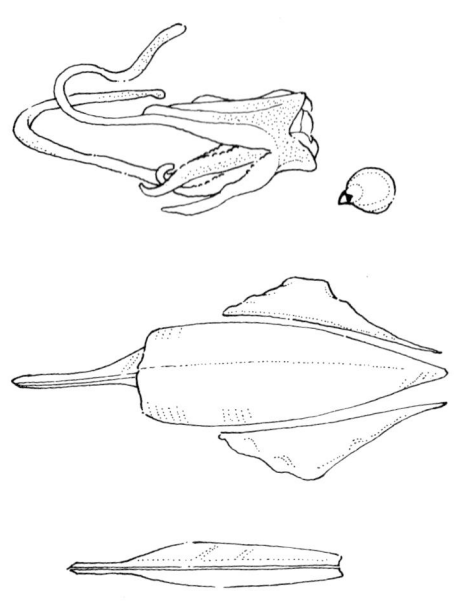

TYPES OF BRAAI EQUIPMENT

There is a wide variety of braai equipment available today, ranging from disposable braai packs to the sophisticated skottelbraais and kettlebraais. The simplest braai is the do-it-yourself one, which includes anything from a pit filled with driftwood to a grid on bricks.

Portable braais: These are useful for beach meals and include the simple disposable braai pack — a small aluminium container, complete with charcoal; the Hibachi braai, which has a cast-iron base with adjustable vents for temperature control and an adjustable grid; picnic braais, which fold up into a case and are available in various shapes and sizes, some with rotisserie and kebab attachments; and the well-known open braziers, most of which have wheels and adjustable grids, and some of which have half-hoods for wind protection. Other equipment gaining popularity, especially on beaches where fires are prohibited, are gas braais like the skottelbraai (which is ideal for stir-fries), the smoker cooker (for smoking fish and seafood) and the recently introduced gas braai oven. Kettlebraais (covered grills) have a large fire-bowl in which coals are laid. The lid can close completely, reflecting heat inwards so that food cooks on both sides simultaneously. There are adjustable dampers in the base to control temperature. Also available are electric braais, which cook food quickly and efficiently.

Built-in braais: These require shelter from prevailing winds and a good draft for the chimney to prevent smoke from billowing everywhere as you braai. Useful features to incorporate are an adjustable grid, a large working surface and a storage place for wood or charcoal. Currently popular are pizza ovens which offer the convenience of 'baking' while enjoying the outdoors.

BRAAI UTENSILS

Use a *hinged* grid or a specially designed *fish basket* for braaiing whole fish, as these prevent the fish from breaking apart when it is turned. Fish in foil braaied on an open grid can be turned with a pair of *long-handled tongs*. An *egg lifter* is ideal for turning ingredients cooked on a griddle or skottelbraai. A *wire brush* is useful for cleaning the grid before and after braaiing, and coals can be moved with a scissor-like pair of *short tongs*. Use *long-handled basting brushes* to baste fish and seafood with oils and marinades; do not use a brush with plastic bristles which will melt. Use *wooden or bamboo skewers* for fish and seafood kebabs. Metal ones are difficult to handle when hot and sometimes burn the food. A *flame-proof apron* and a pair of *gloves*, padded on both sides, will protect you from flying sparks and possible burns.

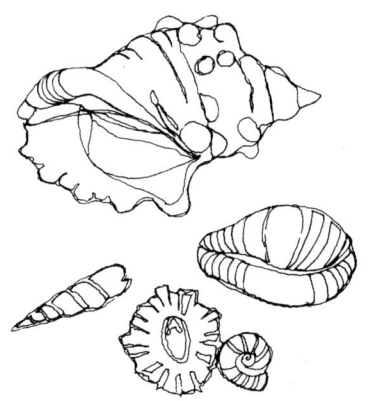

PREPARING THE FIRE

Fuel: The quality and quantity of fuel plays an important role in ensuring the success of the braai. Charcoal, which is available in briquettes or pieces, provides constant heat and burns for longer than wood. Popular types of wood include leadwood, karee and ironwood (all make hot coals) and hook thorn and rooikrans (moderate coals). Do not use tamboti or oleander woods, which give off poisonous fumes, or pine and gum woods, which impart an unpleasant, resinous flavour to food. Avoid using young, green wood or any wood that has been painted, sealed or chemically treated.

Starting the fire: The simplest way to start the fire is to crumple up a few sheets of newspaper, sprinkle them with 1–2 pieces of broken-up fire-lighter or a handful of fire-lighter granules (do not use too much or the food will smell of paraffin), and pack dry twigs upright over them. Light the fire-lighter and add more twigs until the fire is burning steadily. Add solid fuel — dry wood, briquettes or charcoal pieces — and build up a strong fire, then allow it to burn down to hot coals. Spread the coals out slightly to create a larger cooking surface and place the grid over them.

Preparing the grid: Heat it in the fire and scrape off any charred matter with a wire brush. Coat the grid with oil to prevent the food from sticking to it.

Temperature control: Fish has delicate flesh that will burn easily if the coals are too hot. It is best to braai fish and seafood on a grid 10 cm above low coals. If your coals are moderate heat, raise the grid level to 15 cm above them. To judge the temperature of the fire, use the following simple guidelines:
- Hot coals are an ashy colour (45 minutes for a charcoal fire; 1 hour for a wood fire).
- Moderate coals are covered with ash (1 hour for a charcoal fire; 1½ hours for a wood fire).
- Low coals are covered with a thick layer of ash (1¼ hours for a charcoal fire; 1¾ hours for a wood fire).

To vary the cooking temperature during braaiing, you can raise or lower the grid level, or remove coals to lower the temperature, and add more to raise it.

Timing: Fish is cooked when the thickest part of the flesh is white and opaque in the middle. As a rough guide:
- A 2,5-cm thick fish fillet will cook in about 10 minutes.
- A whole fish on the grid will cook in 15–20 minutes per 500 g.
- Fish wrapped in foil will cook over the coals in 20–25 minutes per 500 g.

COOKING

Braaiing a whole fish: Use a fish basket to make it easier to turn a whole fish, or butterfly the fish and use a hinged grid. If cooking the fish unskinned, make incisions in the skin to prevent the flesh from bursting out. Always baste fish well before and during braaiing. With butterflied fish, braai the skin side first, then briefly braai the flesh side.

Fish in foil: Use heavy-duty foil, shiny side in to reflect heat inwards. Oil the foil, wrap it around the fish and place parcel either on the braai or in the coals.

Stir-frying fish and seafood: Heat a little oil in a skottelbraai and stir-fry briefly.

Fish and seafood on skewers: Thread chunks of firm-fleshed fish and seafood onto skewers, with or without vegetables, and cook quickly over moderate coals, turning and basting often.

Soups & Starters

The next time you invite friends over for a braai, prepare a soup or starter over the coals or in the pizza oven or in the skottelbraai or kettlebraai, and serve it as a tasty alternative to the usual bowl of crisps to keep the hunger pangs at bay while you are preparing the main course.

You probably don't think of soup as a dish to prepare over the coals, because it often requires a good deal of preparation and cooking time. As a first course at a braai, it certainly does not seem worth the time and trouble. However, the recipes given in this chapter show that soup is simple to prepare over the coals or in the pizza oven.

A starter is usually only on the menu at a more formal dinner party, but it need not be an elaborate dish that takes hours to prepare. The starters given here cater for a wide range of tastes and occasions, from simple and wholesome snacks to light and elegant delicacies, and are all relatively easy and quick to prepare.

Fresh fish and seafood from our bountiful waters: crayfish, harders, red stumpnose and red roman.

Soups

The delectable fishy soups given here are colourful and tasty and so easy to prepare that you will want to make them all the time.

Bouillabaisse Over the Coals

A South African version of the Marseilles classic, brought right up to date with a touch of spice and herbs. If you wish, serve it in the French manner with Rouille (a garlic sauce); our version — Hot Garlic and Anchovy Sauce — is on page 36. Or be authentic and serve the soup with crisp slices of Olive and Anchovy Crostini (page 15).

50 ml olive or sunflower oil
2 onions, thinly sliced
2 leeks, well washed and thinly sliced
4 medium potatoes, peeled and cubed
3 cloves garlic, crushed
4 large ripe tomatoes, skinned and chopped
a few sprigs fresh fennel
3 sprigs fresh parsley
2 ml turmeric
1,5 litres fish stock
250 ml dry white wine
salt and milled black pepper to taste
1 kg yellowtail, filleted, skinned and cubed
12 prawns
250 g calamari, sliced
6 cooked mussels on the shell

Heat oil in a large cast-iron pot over the coals and sauté the onions, leeks and potatoes until onions are transparent — about 5–10 minutes. Stir in the crushed garlic and chopped tomatoes, simmer for 5–10 minutes, then add the herbs, turmeric, fish stock, wine and seasoning. Cook for 15 minutes, then add the fish, prawns and calamari and cook for another 15 minutes. Serve garnished with the mussels, and accompanied by slices of Crostini (page 15).
SERVES 6

Crusty Tomato Soup with Mixed Seafood

Nothing could be easier — or quicker — to make than this tasty tomato soup, but it will win you a chorus of approval. If you don't have a pizza oven, bake the crust in a conventional oven at 200 °C.

3 x 425-g cans good-quality cream of tomato soup
10 ml chopped fresh tarragon or 5 ml dried
1 clove garlic, crushed
pinch sugar
salt and milled black pepper to taste
500 ml milk
200 g frozen marinara mix, cooked
400 g frozen puff pastry

Combine all ingredients except the pastry in a cast-iron pot and heat to boiling point over the coals. When boiling, remove from the coals and pour the soup into six oven-proof soup bowls (stoneware is best) and leave to cool slightly. Roll out the pastry and cut out discs slightly larger than the circumference of the bowls. Wet the edges of the bowls with water, then cover soup with discs of pastry, pressing pastry firmly to the edge of the bowls. Bake in a pizza oven until the crust has puffed up and is golden. Serve immediately.
SERVES 6

Curried Snoek Soup

A variation on the typical West Coast dish, which uses snoek heads to prepare an aromatic fish stock. This version is much quicker and easier to make, but just as tasty.

15 ml sunflower oil
2 large onions, thinly sliced
1 small piece fresh ginger, crushed
3 cloves garlic, crushed
125 ml thinly sliced celery
2 potatoes, peeled and cubed
125 ml cake flour
10 ml salt
1,25 litres fish stock or water
5 ml turmeric
15 ml curry powder
1–2 chillies, seeded and chopped (optional)
1 small snoek, filleted and cut into portions

Heat oil in a cast-iron pot over the coals and sauté onions until transparent — for 5–10 minutes. Add ginger, garlic, celery and potatoes, remove pot from coals and blend in flour to form a smooth paste. Add salt and fish stock or water, stirring constantly. Return pot to the coals and simmer, covered, for 10 minutes, stirring occasionally. Mix the turmeric and curry powder to a smooth paste with a little water and add to soup with the chillies (if using), stirring constantly. Add the snoek and simmer, covered, for 30 minutes. Serve the soup immediately, accompanied by slices of fresh wholewheat bread.
SERVES 6

CRAYFISH, MUSSEL AND SAUSAGE GUMBO

In the deep South of the USA, they make gumbo as a stew, and it always includes okra in the list of ingredients. Our version is an easy-to-make chunky soup that is every bit as good as the original. Using canned tomatoes cuts down on preparation time, but you can also use skinned fresh tomatoes if you wish. Although smoked Vienna sausages are suitable, the fuller flavour of Russian sausages is perhaps better suited to this soup.

15 ml sunflower oil
500 g smoked sausage, cut into 1-cm thick slices
60 ml cake flour
1,5 litres fish stock or water
1 red sweet pepper, seeded and chopped
250 g onions, thinly sliced
1 bay leaf
1 kg cooked crayfish flesh (tail, or legs and body)
16 black mussels, cooked and shelled
400-g can tomatoes, chopped
5 ml chopped fresh thyme
5 ml chopped fresh oregano
2 ml cayenne pepper
5 ml salt
extra cooked seafood (optional)

Heat the oil in a large cast-iron pot over the coals, brown the sausages, then transfer them to a bowl with a slotted spoon. Pour off the fat from the pot and reserve about 30 ml. Make a roux with the flour and the reserved oil, stirring constantly until the mixture is light brown and creamy. Bring the stock to the boil in the cast-iron pot over the coals, stir in the roux mixture, sausages and the rest of the ingredients (except the extra cooked seafood, if using), and boil for about 10 minutes, or until the soup is cooked through and creamy. Add extra cooked seafood to garnish, if desired.
SERVES 6

Crusty Tomato Soup with Mixed Seafood (page 10), Olive and Anchovy Crostini (page 15) and Bouillabaisse over the Coals (page 10).

STARTERS

Here is a delicious selection of recipes for a first course with an interesting variety of fish and seafood as the main theme.

MARINATED TUNA, CARPACCIO STYLE

This is an excellent starter, light yet elegant and — best of all — very easy to prepare the day before and be ready to serve at the braai. The tuna must be very cold, almost frozen, to enable you to slice it thinly enough. If fresh dill is not available, the dried dill tops are the next best thing.

MARINADE
125 ml olive oil
50 ml red wine vinegar
50 ml soy sauce
7 ml salt
5 ml milled black pepper
5 ml fresh dill or dried dill tops
1 large onion, minced
2 cloves garlic, crushed
5 ml capers

500 g filleted tuna, sliced paper thin
lemon wedges

MARINADE: Mix all the ingredients together and set aside for 15 minutes.
Arrange tuna slices on a platter, slightly overlapping. Brush with marinade every few minutes until half the marinade has been used, returning fish to refrigerator after each brushing. Leave overnight, then repeat the following morning, until the fish has absorbed almost all the marinade. Serve with a garnish of lemon wedges and accompanied by crisp French bread.
SERVES 6

MEDALLIONS OF YELLOWTAIL WITH MUSHROOMS

Yellowtail is a marvellous fish on the braai, and prepared this way — packed with mushrooms and garlic and wrapped in foil — the tasty morsels are definitely 'moreish'.

6 filleted yellowtail cutlets, taken from near the tail
200 g black mushrooms, coarsely chopped
2 cloves garlic, crushed
100 g butter, softened
10 ml whole-grain mustard
salt and milled black pepper to taste
fresh coriander or parsley sprigs

Place each yellowtail cutlet on a square of foil, shiny side up, and top with mushrooms. Beat together the garlic, butter and mustard and divide between parcels. Season with salt and pepper and close parcels securely. Braai over moderate coals for 15–20 minutes, or until fish is cooked. Serve immediately, garnished with sprigs of coriander.
SERVES 6

CALAMARI MEDLEY

The rings are deep-fried in the skottelbraai, and the tubes quickly grilled in a ridged cast-iron frying pan over the coals. The secret, when braaiing or grilling calamari, is to cook it quickly. If cooked for too long, the rings and tubes shrivel up and become as tough as old boot leather.

250 g calamari rings
salt and milled black pepper to taste
30 ml cake flour
1 egg, lightly beaten
60 ml very fine dry breadcrumbs
sunflower oil for deep-frying
100 ml melted butter
500 g small calamari tubes

First prepare the calamari rings. Combine salt, pepper and flour in a bowl and dust rings with the mixture. Then dip the rings in beaten egg, then in breadcrumbs, coating completely. Refrigerate for about 30 minutes to set the crumbs. Deep-fry calamari rings *briefly* in heated oil in the skottelbraai, or until crisp, and then remove with a slotted spoon.
Heat a ridged cast-iron frying pan over the coals and brush with melted butter. Brush calamari tubes with melted butter and fry *very quickly* on both sides until opaque — about 2 minutes.
Serve calamari rings and tubes with a selection of dipping sauces (pages 36–37) and flavoured butters (page 40).
SERVES 6

Whole Sardines with Mustard Sauce

Fresh sardines, if you can get them, are delectable cooked over the braai this way. Alternatively, use the frozen pre-packed ones and thaw them partially before use. The batter is a useful one for small fish or seafood, and is really light. Fry the fish in a skottelbraai, or use a cast-iron frying pan and cook them over the coals. The oil should be deep enough to nearly cover the fish.

1 kg fresh sardines, cleaned

BATTER
1 large egg
125 ml milk
125 ml cake flour
salt and milled black pepper to taste

sunflower oil for deep-frying

MUSTARD SAUCE
75 ml sugar
4 eggs
30 ml mustard powder
15 ml cake flour
5 ml salt
5 ml milled black pepper
250 ml red wine vinegar

Pat the sardines dry with a paper towel or a dish cloth. Set aside.
BATTER: Beat egg and milk together, then beat in the flour and season well.
Dip sardines in the batter. Heat the oil in a cast-iron frying pan over the coals and fry sardines for 1–2 minutes on each side (depending on size of fish). Drain on absorbent paper.
MUSTARD SAUCE: Beat 65 ml sugar and the eggs together in cast-iron pot. Combine remaining sugar with the mustard powder, flour, salt and pepper. Add vinegar to this mixture, then stir into the egg mixture in the pot. Heat slowly over the coals, beating continuously until the sauce thickens. Remove from heat. Serve sauce drizzled over sardines, or separately.
SERVES 6

VARIATIONS
Instead of sardines, use 6 small harders or 6 whole calamari. Prepare in the same way as the sardines.

Smoked Salmon Trout with Melba Toast

Use the kettlebraai or a gas smoker-cooker to smoke the trout, or follow the simple do-it-yourself method given here.

1 kg whole salmon trout, cleaned and trimmed
salt and milled black pepper to taste
a few sprigs fennel
12–18 slices Melba toast
butter to serve with toast

Open out the salmon trout and dust with salt and milled pepper, inside and out. Place fennel sprigs inside fish cavity and close up the fish.
To prepare braai, let the fire burn down to coals covered lightly with grey ash.
Soak 125 ml untreated oak shavings in water for 30 minutes and drain well. Sprinkle the shavings in the base of a large flat-based cast-iron pot and place a trivet in the pot. Place the fish on a foil dish and place the dish on the trivet. Cover the pot tightly with the lid and leave the fish to smoke over hot coals for 12 minutes, then over moderate coals (or raise the grid) for another 12 minutes.
Remove the fish from the pot, peel off the skin and serve immediately with slices of Melba toast and curls of butter.
SERVES 6

Chilli Grilled Mussels

If you prefer, simply steam and serve the mussels without the flavoured butter. Winkles (periwinkles), now available commercially in South Africa, may be steamed in the same way as the mussels. Fresh oysters may also be cooked in this way, but use sparkling wine instead of the white wine.

mussels (allow 12–18 per person)
200 ml white wine
5 drops chilli or Tabasco sauce
50 ml butter
30 ml finely chopped fresh parsley
pinch salt

Clean the mussels, then place in a cast-iron pot with the white wine. Add water to cover and steam over the coals, covered, until the shells open — about 5 minutes. Discard any mussels that have not opened. Break off the top half of the shells, leaving mussels on the bottom half. Whip the chilli sauce into the butter and combine with the parsley and salt. Spread this butter mixture on the mussels. Place them, shell side down, on a fine mesh grid and grill them over the coals until the butter has melted. Serve the mussels immediately.
SERVES 6

VARIATION
Instead of using chilli or Tabasco sauce, crush 4 cloves of garlic and combine them with the butter and parsley. Sprinkle the buttered mussels with Parmesan cheese to taste and proceed as described above.

Frikkadel Kebabs

Old-fashioned fish cakes in a new guise — and so easy to make too! Instead of white fish, you can use canned tuna, salmon or pilchards, or any left-over cooked fish.

750 g cooked white fish, finely flaked, or raw minced fish
1 onion, finely chopped or minced
1 slice white bread, crusts removed, soaked in a little milk
1 egg, beaten
30 ml finely chopped fresh parsley
5 ml salt
2 ml milled black pepper
cake flour
sunflower oil for deep-frying
Hot Garlic and Anchovy Sauce (page 36)

Combine the fish, onion, white bread, egg, parsley and seasoning. Roll the mixture into small balls and dust with a little flour. Heat the oil in a skottelbraai and drop the fish frikkadels into the oil. Fry until cooked — about 5 minutes. Remove the frikkadels from the oil with a slotted spoon and drain them on absorbent paper. Thread the frikkadels onto bamboo skewers to form kebabs. Serve the kebabs with Hot Garlic and Anchovy Sauce drizzled over them, or serve the sauce separately.
SERVES 6

CROSTINI

The most basic version of this Italian-style snack is a thick slice of Peasant Bread (page 43) rubbed with garlic, toasted over the coals and then drizzled with olive oil while still hot.

6–12 thick slices of coarse bread or French bread

OLIVE AND ANCHOVY
150 g pitted black olives
4 anchovies, chopped or mashed
30 ml capers, squeezed to discard vinegar
1–2 cloves garlic, crushed
75 ml olive oil
finely chopped fresh parsley

TOMATO AND ONION
1–2 large ripe tomatoes, sliced
1 large onion, sliced into rings
6–12 sardines or smoked mussels
75 ml olive oil
2 cloves garlic, crushed

TOMATO, BASIL AND MOZZARELLA
75 ml olive oil
1–2 large ripe tomatoes, sliced
6–12 thick slices mozzarella cheese
6–12 fresh basil leaves

Toast slices of bread on one side.
OLIVE AND ANCHOVY: Place all ingredients except the parsley in a food processor or blender and chop coarsely. Spread onto untoasted side of bread. Grill in a pizza oven or kettlebraai (with lid closed) until bubbling. Sprinkle parsley over and serve.
TOMATO AND ONION: Arrange sliced tomato and onion on top of untoasted side of bread and top each slice with a sardine. Drizzle olive oil over and sprinkle with crushed garlic. Cook in a pizza oven, or in a kettlebraai, until bubbling.
TOMATO, BASIL AND MOZZARELLA: Brush untoasted side of bread with olive oil and toast again. Top each slice of bread with a slice of tomato and mozzarella and grill in a pizza oven or kettlebraai until cheese melts. Garnish with basil leaves.
Serve immediately.
SERVES 6

Marinated Tuna, Carpaccio Style (page 12), Chilli Grilled Mussels (page 13) and Sweet Peppers with Anchovy Dressing (this page).

SWEET PEPPERS WITH ANCHOVY DRESSING

This easy starter salad combines the bright colours of the peppers with a delightfully sharp dressing. If you don't like anchovies, you can use canned smoked mussels or oysters.

4 sweet peppers (red, green, yellow and black)

DRESSING
6–8 anchovy fillets, finely chopped
1–2 cloves garlic, crushed
20 ml finely chopped capers
a few sprigs fresh oregano, finely chopped
100 ml olive oil

Char the peppers over hot coals, then place immediately in a plastic bag, close tightly and leave for 10 minutes to loosen skins. Peel peppers, quarter each pepper, and discard seeds. Arrange on a large serving platter or on individual dishes.
DRESSING: Mix ingredients in a screw-top jar. Pour over peppers to serve.
SERVES 6

BRAAIED HARDERS

Traditionally, harders are served with borriepatats — a yellow-fleshed sweet potato that is delectable topped with butter and cinnamon.

GARLIC OIL
125 ml sunflower oil
2 cloves garlic, crushed

6 fresh harders, cleaned and gutted
salt and milled black pepper to taste

GARLIC OIL: Heat oil slightly in a skillet over the coals, add garlic and sauté until transparent. Remove from heat, and leave to stand for about 10 minutes. Remove garlic with a slotted spoon.
Brush harders with the oil. Season to taste, inside and out, and braai over coals until cooked to taste — about 10 minutes on each side. Serve with borriepatats.
SERVES 6

STARTERS • 15

Fish & Seafood

Main-course fish and seafood dishes, cooked over the coals, in a kettlebraai or skottelbraai, in the pizza oven or on a griddle are the theme of this chapter. The ever-popular potjiekos has not been forgotten either. The wide range of cooking methods that are used is testament to South Africans' dedication to outdoor cooking, never mind the weather, and this selection of recipes will tantalize your taste-buds and make outdoor cooking and entertaining more popular than it already is.
Freshly caught fish and seafood, simply prepared and grilled over the coals on the beach is the perfect way to savour the fresh taste of the sea. It is also fun to experiment judiciously with flavours for a taste adventure. The collection of delicious dishes in this chapter cater for most types of fish and seafood found in South African oceans and inland waters, but also include suggestions for using the convenience of frozen or canned fish and seafood.

Pot Bread (page 43); a springer harder and yellowtail; Mussel Potjie (page 28); a pair of red roman; and Line Fish in Newspaper (page 20).

Fish

Explore the piquant diversity of flavours offered; there is a dish to suit every occasion — from the informality of fish burgers to the elegance of sole Kiev.

Fish Thermidor

Crayfish is the usual seafood graced with thermidor sauce, but in these days of high seafood prices, cheaper hake or angelfish make tasty alternatives.

SAUCE
50 ml butter
45 ml cake flour
250 ml milk
250 ml cream
10 ml hot English mustard
20 ml Worcestershire sauce
pinch cayenne pepper or peri-peri powder
salt and milled black pepper to taste
125 ml grated Gruyère cheese
125 ml brandy or sherry

2 kg cooked hake or angelfish fillets, cubed

TOPPING
100 ml very finely grated Cheddar cheese
butter

SAUCE: Melt the butter in a cast-iron pot, then remove from the heat and stir in the flour to make a paste. Add the milk, cream, mustard, Worcestershire sauce, cayenne pepper and seasoning. Stir over low heat until thickened and smooth — for about 3 minutes. Remove from the heat and stir in the cheese and brandy.
Place the fish cubes in an oven-proof dish and pour the sauce over. Top with grated Cheddar cheese and dot with butter. Bake in a pizza oven for about 30 minutes, or until the dish is heated through and bubbling. Serve immediately.
SERVES 6

Whole Stuffed Geelbek in Foil

Hake, kingklip or line fish can also be cooked this way.

1 whole geelbek, gutted
10 ml salt

STUFFING
250 ml fresh white breadcrumbs
1 egg, beaten
5 ml very finely chopped onion
10 ml very finely chopped fresh parsley
5 ml very finely chopped fresh basil
milled black pepper to taste
2 ml salt

30 g dry breadcrumbs
30 ml butter or margarine

Sprinkle fish with the 10 ml salt.
STUFFING: Mix all ingredients together and use to stuff cavity of fish.
Secure fish with skewers or string and place in a large oven-proof dish lined with foil. Sprinkle dry breadcrumbs over fish and dot with butter or margarine. Bake in a pizza oven or a kettlebraai (with the lid closed) for 30–40 minutes, depending on size of fish. Serve immediately.
SERVES 6–8

Rainbow Trout with Almond Butter

Salmon trout, elf and springers can also be prepared this way. Carp are also good, but need a lot of pre-preparation.

BUTTER
100 g butter, softened
75 ml ground almonds
2 drops almond essence

STUFFING
3 bacon rashers, chopped and fried crisply
75 ml ground almonds
45 ml chopped fresh chives
1 onion, finely chopped
750 ml fresh breadcrumbs
75 ml natural yoghurt or sour cream

6 whole trout, gutted and boned

BUTTER: Mix butter with almonds and essence and form into a roll. Chill until firm. (Or don't roll and chill butter but drop a little onto each piece of stuffed fish.)
STUFFING: Combine all the ingredients well. Stuff cavities in fish with the stuffing.
Secure fish with skewers or toothpicks and place on pieces of buttered foil. Cut chilled butter into 6 slices. Top each piece of fish with a slice of butter. Close foil securely and braai fish over moderate coals until tender — for 30–40 minutes. Serve immediately, accompanied by Herbed Baby Potato Salad (page 33).
SERVES 6

Tuna with Peppercorn Crust (page 20), Game Fish Steaks with Olives and Tomatoes (page 21) and Salt Snoek Kedgeree (page 24).

FISH • 19

Red Roman with Piquant Yoghurt Sauce

Yellowtail, geelbek, hake and kingklip can all be prepared in this way and served with yoghurt sauce.

SAUCE
200–250 ml natural yoghurt
50–60 ml mayonnaise
30 ml chopped parsley
2 ml chopped fresh dill or 1 ml dried
salt and milled black pepper to taste

6 red roman cutlets
salt and milled black pepper to taste
75 ml melted butter

SAUCE: Mix ingredients together and refrigerate until needed.
Season the fish with salt and pepper, brush with melted butter and place in a hinged grid. Braai over moderate coals for 10–15 minutes, or until cooked. Serve with the yoghurt sauce.
SERVES 6

Tuna with Peppercorn Crust

Fillet steak is prepared this way, and tuna flesh is so firm that it is ideal for the same treatment. You could also try game fish steaks, like tunny or leervis.

6 yellowfin tuna steaks
melted butter
10 ml salt
60 ml black peppercorns, coarsely ground
sunflower oil

Brush the tuna steaks with melted butter. Season them with salt and then press ground peppercorns into both sides of the steaks, using your hands. Chill the steaks in the refrigerator to set the peppercorn crust. Brush a griddle with sunflower oil, then grill the steaks over the coals for 7–10 minutes on each side, or until they are done. Serve the steaks accompanied by Fresh Tomato Sauce (page 36).
SERVES 6

Baby Kabeljou with Tomato and Rosemary Butter

Whole baby hake is a cheaper — but just as tasty — alternative to the baby kabeljou.

6 whole baby kabeljou, filleted
salt and milled black pepper to taste
melted butter or sunflower oil
6 sprigs fresh rosemary

TOMATO AND ROSEMARY BUTTER
100 ml butter
10 ml tomato paste
milled black pepper to taste
10 ml finely chopped fresh rosemary
2 ml ground paprika

Season kabeljou inside and out with salt and pepper. Brush with melted butter or oil and place in a hinged grid. Braai for about 7 minutes on each side.
TOMATO AND ROSEMARY BUTTER: Combine all ingredients well. Form into a roll, wrap in wax paper and chill until firm. Slice and serve on braaied kabeljou, with a garnish of fresh rosemary.
SERVES 6

Line Fish in Banana Leaves

This is the perfect way to braai freshly caught fish on the beach.

1–2 whole line fish, gutted
salt to taste
milled black pepper to taste
banana leaves

Wash freshly caught fish well (but leave scales on). Season and wrap in several large banana leaves. Make a fire on the sand and, once it has died down sufficiently to make hot coals, shovel coals aside. Dig a hole in the hot sand and bury the wrapped fish. Cover with a layer of hot sand about 5 cm deep. Shovel coals on top of sand, covering fish, and leave until cooked — about 45–60 minutes, depending on size of fish. Dig out fish, discard leaves, skin and scale fish and serve.
SERVES 6

Line Fish in Newspaper

As a variation, the wrapped fish can be cooked on coals buried in the sand.

2–2,5 kg line fish of your choice, cleaned
15 ml salt
2 cloves garlic, crushed
10 ml chopped fresh parsley or dill
20 ml butter or margarine

Season the fish inside and out with salt. Mix the garlic with the parsley and butter and spread inside the cavity of the fish. Wrap the fish in 10–12 soaking wet sheets of newspaper and bury the parcel in moderate coals, heaping some coals on top. Cook for 30–40 minutes, or until tender. Serve immediately.
SERVES 6

Smoorvis

This can also be cooked in a cast-iron potjie over the coals or in an oven-proof dish in the pizza oven.

1 kg cooked snoek
30 ml sunflower oil
15 ml butter or margarine
1 large onion, chopped
2 cloves garlic, crushed
2 large potatoes, cubed
2 medium tomatoes, skinned and chopped
1 small green pepper, seeded and sliced or chopped
5 ml salt
2 ml milled black pepper

Flake fish and remove bones. Heat oil and butter in a skottelbraai and sauté onion and garlic until transparent. Add potatoes and sauté until starting to soften, stirring often. Add tomatoes, green pepper and snoek. Simmer until heated through, then season and mix well. Serve with hot rice.
SERVES 6

VARIATIONS
Use smoked snoek instead of fresh, or use a salted snoek, first soaked in cold water for 1 hour to remove salt.

Wine-Baked Geelbek

1 kg geelbek fillets, cut into portions
5 ml salt
milled black pepper to taste
50 ml butter
1 onion, sliced
about 10 mange-tout, trimmed
2 carrots, peeled and cut into julienne strips
300 ml dry white wine
1 bouquet garni (parsley, thyme, bay leaf)
15 ml cake flour
lemon wedges
sprigs of fresh parsley

Season the fish with salt and pepper. Melt half the butter in a flat-based cast-iron pot or frying pan over the coals and sauté the onion, mange-tout and carrots until the onion is transparent and the other vegetables are golden. Place the fish portions on top, pour the wine over and add the bouquet garni. Cover the pot with a tight-fitting lid and poach the fish gently over low coals or at the edge of the fire for 25 minutes or until the fish flakes easily. Mix the cake flour to a paste with a little of the hot poaching liquid, then stir in the remaining butter. Add, bit by bit, to the poaching liquid to thicken it slightly. Serve immediately with lemon wedges, and a garnish of parsley sprigs.
SERVES 6

Spicy Crumbed Fish Bites

These delectable morsels are perfect with Hot Garlic and Anchovy Sauce (page 36). Or serve them with Garlic Butter Sauce (page 36) as a dip.

1 kg filleted firm-fleshed fish, cubed
cake flour
1 egg, beaten

COATING
200 ml dry breadcrumbs
5 ml curry powder
5 ml salt
milled black pepper to taste

sunflower oil for deep-frying

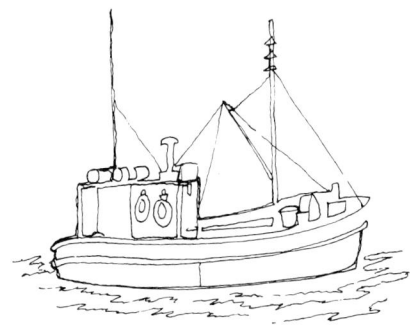

Dust fish cubes with cake flour, then dip in beaten egg, covering completely. Combine all the coating ingredients in a bowl and roll fish cubes in it. Refrigerate to set coating. Heat the oil in a skottelbraai or a flat-bottomed cast-iron pot over the coals and deep-fry cubes until golden — about 5 minutes. Drain on absorbent paper and serve immediately, accompanied by Hot Garlic and Anchovy Sauce (page 36).
SERVES 6

VARIATIONS
Use chilli or peri-peri powder instead of the curry powder.

Game Fish Steaks with Olives and Tomatoes

This very easy dish can either be baked in the pizza oven or fried in a cast-iron frying pan over the coals.

a little olive or sunflower oil
6 firm-fleshed game fish steaks (such as tuna, marlin, swordfish)
salt and milled black pepper to taste
100 g pitted black olives, chopped
20 ml capers
4 large ripe tomatoes, skinned and chopped
chopped fresh basil to taste

Brush a ceramic dish — or a large cast-iron frying pan — with oil and place the game fish steaks in it. Season lightly and sprinkle olives, capers, tomatoes and basil over. Sprinkle with a little olive oil and bake in a pizza oven for 20–30 minutes, or fry over the coals for 20 minutes or until the flesh flakes easily, turning once.
SERVES 6

Salmon Trout Parcels

The wine-soaked baking parchment gives a tasty, moist result. River trout may also be used.

6 pieces baking parchment
100 ml dry white or rosé wine
6 salmon trout steaks
7 ml fennel or dill seeds
45 ml butter
salt and milled black pepper to taste
fresh dill sprigs

Crush the pieces of parchment together, place in a small bowl and pour the wine over. Leave to soak for 1 hour, pushing down into the bowl occasionally. Separate and open out parchment sheets and place a salmon trout steak on each. Sprinkle fennel or dill over and dot with butter. Season to taste and drizzle any remaining wine over. Lift up opposite sides of baking parchment and fold them together, twist and tuck under two shorter ends. Place parcels on a baking sheet and bake in a pizza oven or kettlebraai (with closed lid) for about 15 minutes, or until fish flakes easily. Serve at once, garnished with sprigs of fresh dill.
SERVES 6

Butterflied Snoek

Freshly caught galjoen — if you can get it — may also be prepared in this way.

1 whole fresh snoek, entrails removed
melted butter or margarine
15 ml salt
5 ml milled black pepper
lemon juice

Wash the snoek well and pat dry. Butterfly fish (page 5), then brush with melted butter and season inside and out. Sprinkle a little lemon juice inside cavity and place fish, skin side down, on grid (a hinged grid for easier turning). Braai over hot coals for 3 minutes on each side, then raise grid to 30 cm above coals and braai for 15 minutes on each side. Baste often with butter.
SERVES 6–8

Kabeljou Provençale

Kabeljou lends itself to cooking with tomatoes and garlic, in the provençale way. Also good prepared this way are any kind of firm-fleshed fish (such as angelfish, tuna, snoek, kingklip, yellowtail and geelbek).

30 ml olive or sunflower oil
200 ml finely chopped onion
2 cloves garlic, crushed
750 g plum tomatoes, skinned, seeded and chopped
4 anchovy fillets, drained and finely chopped
125 ml dry white wine
1 ml cayenne pepper
5 ml crumbled dried thyme
750 g kabeljou fillets or cutlets
175 ml chopped black olives
5 ml capers
salt and milled black pepper to taste
15 ml finely chopped fresh basil

Heat the oil in a skottelbraai and sauté the onions until they are transparent. Add the garlic and cook, stirring, for half a minute. Add the chopped tomatoes and anchovies and cook over fairly high heat, stirring, for 5 minutes. Add the wine, cayenne pepper and thyme and bring to the boil, stirring. Add the fish cutlets and cook them for 5–10 minutes on either side, or until tender and easy to flake with a fork. Transfer the fish to a heated platter and keep warm, covered, at the edge of the braai fire while you make the sauce.

Bring the cooking liquor to a full boil and stir over high heat until slightly thickened. Add the olives, capers, salt and pepper and simmer for 2 minutes. Spoon the sauce over the fish and sprinkle the basil over. Serve immediately.
SERVES 4–6

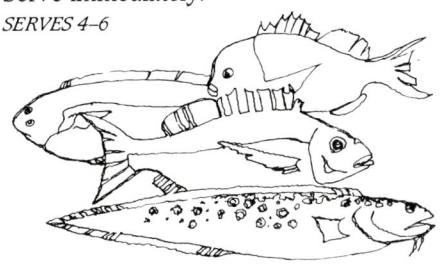

Whole Stuffed Geelbek in Foil (page 18), Corn and Tomato Salsa (page 34) and Seafood Pizza (page 29).

Skate Wings with Blue Cheese

The flesh on the skate wings remains delightfully moist, and goes particularly well with the flavour of the blue cheese. Skate is not a very expensive fish, and is one which perhaps deserves to be better known.

6 skate wings
garlic powder to taste
salt and milled black pepper to taste
sunflower oil for frying
finely grated blue cheese or other mature cheese to taste

Dust the skate wings on both sides with garlic powder, salt and pepper. Brush a skottelbraai or griddle with sunflower oil, then cook the skate wings for about 5 minutes on each side. Remove skate wings from braai, sprinkle grated cheese over and serve immediately.
SERVES 6

VARIATIONS
Instead of serving with the grated cheese, use one of the savoury butters on page 40. Another interesting variation is to use marmalade or mint jelly as a topping.

Braaied Garlic Angelfish

This is definitely the most aromatic way to braai angelfish, and, served with potatoes and mushrooms baked in sour cream, it is a dish fit for the gods. As a bonus, it is not at all expensive.

2 angelfish, gutted
salt and milled black pepper to taste
garlic powder to taste
melted butter or margarine

Dust the cavity of the fish with salt and pepper, and garlic powder. Brush with melted butter. Braai the fish over moderate coals for 45 minutes, turning often, or until the skin begins to lift from fish. Remove the skin and cut off fish fillets. Serve fish accompanied by baked potatoes and mushrooms cooked in sour cream.
SERVES 6

FISH • 23

Salt Snoek Kedgeree with Brown Rice

Haddock or kippers are generally used to make breakfast kedgeree. This version uses inexpensive salted snoek for an individual flavour.

400 g salted snoek
50 ml water
50 ml milk
5 ml mild curry powder
75 ml butter or margarine
2 ml milled black pepper
500 ml cooked brown rice
3 hard-boiled eggs, shelled and coarsely chopped
50 ml chopped fresh parsley
1 hard-boiled egg, sliced, for garnish

Place the snoek in a shallow flat-bottomed cast-iron pot. Pour over the water and milk, sprinkle with the curry powder, and dot with the butter or margarine. Simmer gently, covered, over low coals until tender — about 15 minutes. Remove fish from pan with a slotted spoon and reserve cooking liquor. Remove skin and bones from snoek and flake flesh coarsely. Add pepper, then mix with the cooked rice, enough of the liquor to moisten, the chopped eggs and parsley in the cast-iron pot. Heat briefly over the coals, then serve immediately, garnished with sliced egg.
SERVES 6

Sole Kiev Parcels

If sole is a bit expensive, use baby hake instead. If you cannot find ricotta cheese, use smooth cottage cheese, but drain it first through a muslin-lined sieve (or coffee filter paper).

6 baby sole fillets
salt and milled black pepper to taste

GARLIC BUTTER STUFFING
60 ml butter
40 ml ricotta or drained smooth cottage cheese
2 cloves garlic, crushed
10 ml chopped fresh chives or 5 ml chopped fresh coriander leaves

Season the soles with salt and pepper. Pat dry with absorbent paper.
GARLIC BUTTER STUFFING: Combine all the ingredients together well.

Spread butter onto fish fillets and roll them up, starting at the tail end. Secure rolls with toothpicks or skewers. Chill for 30–45 minutes. Wrap rolled-up soles in foil (shiny side inside) and cook over moderate coals for 10 minutes, or place parcels on a baking sheet and cook them in the pizza oven or a kettlebraai.
SERVES 6

Tandoori Fish

A marvellous combination of flavours, served to perfection with Sambal Selection (page 34).

MARINADE
30 ml lemon juice
5 ml ground coriander seeds
2 ml crushed cumin seeds
2 ml onion powder
2 cloves garlic, crushed
10 ml peeled and crushed fresh ginger
5 ml salt
2 ml ground cinnamon
2 ml turmeric
5 ml cayenne pepper
200 ml natural yoghurt

1 kg white fish fillets (such as hake, kabeljou, yellowtail, kingklip)
sunflower oil for frying

MARINADE: Combine lemon juice and all the spices and mix well with the yoghurt.
Place the fish fillets in a shallow dish and pour the marinade over. Set aside to marinate for 1–2 hours. Heat a skottelbraai and brush with oil. Remove fish from marinade and cook for 5–10 minutes on either side, or until fish flakes easily. Baste with marinade during cooking. Serve accompanied by couscous or rice.
SERVES 6

Spicy Fish Fritters

Hake works particularly well, but any firm-fleshed white fish may be used to make these fritters.

500 g hake fillets, cut into strips and very finely chopped
250 ml desiccated coconut
3 eggs, lightly beaten
2 spring onions, finely chopped
15 ml cornflour
10 ml ground coriander
15 ml lemon juice
15 ml ground cumin
salt and milled black pepper to taste

BATTER
200 ml cake flour
salt and milled black pepper to taste
2 eggs, separated
50 ml melted butter, cooled
150 ml white wine
150 ml milk or water

a little butter or sunflower oil

Mix fish, coconut, eggs, onions, cornflour, coriander, lemon juice, cumin and seasoning. Chill for 30 minutes.
BATTER: Sift flour, salt and pepper into a bowl and make a well in the centre. Stir in the egg yolks and cooled melted butter, drawing flour in gradually and adding wine a little at a time. Set aside for 1 hour, covered. Stir in milk and fold in stiffly whisked egg whites.

Add fish mixture to batter and fold in lightly. Drop tablespoonfuls of mixture onto a heated, well-greased griddle on top of the coals, or into a greased skottelbraai, and cook for 1–2 minutes on either side, or until golden. Serve immediately.
SERVES 6–8

Fish Burgers on the Braai

These can also be cooked on the griddle over moderate coals. They are a good way to use up left-over cooked fish.

750 ml cooked firm fish, flaked
450 ml mashed potatoes
1 small onion, finely grated
20 ml chopped fresh parsley
20 ml melted butter
2 eggs, separated
salt and milled black pepper to taste
cake flour
sunflower oil for frying

6 hamburger rolls
Tartar Sauce (page 36)
6 fresh tomato slices
a few crisp lettuce leaves

Combine fish, potatoes, onion, parsley and butter. Add the egg yolks and the white of 1 egg and mix well. Beat remaining egg white lightly and set aside. Season fish mixture to taste with salt and pepper, then form into patties. Dip patties in egg white and dust with flour. Refrigerate until firm — about 45 minutes. Heat the oil in a skottelbraai and fry the fish patties until golden — about 5 minutes on each side. Drain on absorbent paper.

Place the fish patties on halved hot hamburger rolls and brush liberally with the Tartar Sauce. Serve the burgers at once, garnished with slices of fresh tomato and crisp lettuce leaves.
SERVES 6

Blackened Fish

The herbs and spices used to season the fish 'blacken' as the fish is grilled to form a tasty coating.

1,5 kg yellowtail or kabeljou fillets
75 ml melted butter
7 ml dried thyme
7 ml dried oregano
5 ml salt
5 ml milled black pepper
5 ml cayenne pepper
7 ml garlic powder
7 ml onion powder

Cut the fish into portions and brush with a little of the melted butter. Heat a cast-iron frying pan over the coals until very hot. Combine the herbs, seasoning and spices and press firmly onto both sides of the fish portions. Fry the fish in the un-oiled frying pan for 5 minutes on either side, or until well blackened, spooning a little extra butter over, if necessary. Add remaining butter to the frying pan and fry fish on both sides until it flakes easily, then serve accompanied by a crisp green salad.
SERVES 6–8

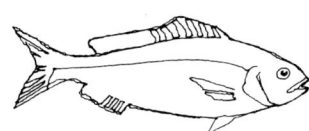

Fish Breyani

An easy version of the Malay classic, that is really quick to make in a cast-iron potjie over the braai fire, if you have cooked rice and cooked lentils at hand. Use whatever fish you fancy — but it must be firm-fleshed.

MARINADE
30 ml breyani mix
5 ml turmeric
3 cloves garlic, crushed
1 small piece fresh ginger, crushed
5 ml salt
250 ml natural yoghurt

1,5 kg firm white fish, cut into portions
125 ml sunflower oil
6 medium potatoes, peeled and cubed
3 medium onions, sliced
750 ml cooked rice
200 ml cooked red lentils
2 tomatoes, skinned and coarsely chopped

MARINADE: Combine marinade ingredients. Pour marinade over the fish and set aside for 10 minutes.

Heat the oil in a cast-iron potjie and brown the potatoes. Add onions and sauté until browned. Cover onions and potatoes in the potjie with a layer each of rice, lentils, tomatoes, and fish and marinade. Cook, covered, over the coals for 30 minutes, or until fish is tender.
SERVES 6

Fish Bobotie

Another Malay favourite deliciously updated by using fish rather than meat. Any firm-fleshed fish may be used.

500 g cooked white fish, skinned and boned
1 thick slice white bread, crusts removed
300 ml milk
65 ml butter or margarine
1 large onion, coarsely chopped
juice of 1 lemon
10 ml curry powder
30 ml seedless raisins
30 ml blanched almonds
5 ml salt
1 ml milled black pepper
2 large eggs
2 bay or lemon leaves

Flake fish into a bowl. Soak bread in milk. Melt butter in a cast-iron frying pan over the coals and sauté onion until transparent. Add lemon juice, curry powder, raisins, almonds, and seasoning and cook for 1 minute. Add fish. Squeeze milk from bread and reserve. Add bread to fish and mix well. Beat eggs, add reserved milk and beat again until well blended. Pour fish mixture into greased oven-proof dish, pour egg and milk mixture over and top with whole bay leaves. Bake in a pizza oven for 35 minutes, or until set. Serve with rice.
SERVES 6

Tuna Noodle Bake

Although time is spent on preparation, this is an easy and inexpensive dish.

750 ml Cheese Sauce (page 37)
300 g ribbon noodles, cooked al dente
2 x 200-g cans tuna in brine, drained and flaked
250 ml grated Cheddar cheese

Add Cheese Sauce to cooked noodles, then stir in tuna. Transfer to a large oven-proof dish, smooth the top and sprinkle with grated cheese. Bake in a pizza oven for 30 minutes, or until bubbling on top.
SERVES 6

SEAFOOD

Whether they are prepared simply or used in more elaborate dishes, our wide variety of seafood is marvellous cooked out of doors.

MEALIE MEAL SEAFOOD FRITTERS

These very easy fritters can be made either in the skottelbraai or on a griddle over the coals.

125 ml cake flour
5 ml sugar
10 ml baking powder
2 ml bicarbonate of soda
2 ml salt
250 ml yellow mealie meal
2 large eggs, lightly beaten
315 ml buttermilk
30 ml melted and cooled butter
3 large spring onions, finely chopped
15 ml very finely chopped fresh parsley
250 ml chopped cooked seafood of your choice (such as prawns, crab meat, mussels, alikreukel, winkles)
pinch cayenne pepper
a little butter or sunflower oil

Sift flour, sugar, baking powder, bicarbonate of soda and salt into the mealie meal. In another bowl, mix eggs, buttermilk and butter. Add to mealie meal mixture and stir until smooth. Set aside for 10 minutes.
Stir the onions, parsley, seafood and cayenne pepper into pancake batter. Lightly grease a skottelbraai or griddle with butter. Drop tablespoonfuls of batter onto skottelbraai or griddle and cook fritters for 1–2 minutes on either side, or until golden. Serve at once.
SERVES 4–6

Marinated Baby Vegetables (page 33) and Seafood Fondue (page 28).

SEAFOOD PILAFF

A delectable mixture of seafood cooked with rice and redolent with herbs.

30 ml sunflower oil or butter
1 large onion, chopped
2 cloves garlic, chopped
½ green sweet pepper, seeded and chopped
2 large ripe tomatoes, skinned and chopped
500 g uncooked rice
1 cube chicken stock, crumbled
1 litre boiling water
2 ml turmeric
milled black pepper to taste
5 ml mixed chopped fresh oregano and savory
2 ml chopped fresh basil
3 crayfish tails, shelled and cut into chunks
250 g calamari tubes, sliced
3 cooked perlemoen, cubed

Heat oil in a flat-based cast-iron pot. Fry onion, garlic, green pepper and tomatoes briefly. Add rice to pot and stir-fry for 2–3 minutes. Dissolve stock cube in water, stir in turmeric, pepper and herbs and pour over rice mixture. Add seafood, cover and simmer over moderate coals until rice is cooked and has swelled up — about 40 minutes. If mixture gets too dry, add more stock or water. Serve immediately.
SERVES 6

SEAFOOD PIES

If you have the time to prepare it, this pie is a delicious and wholesome treat.

FILLING
30 ml olive or sunflower oil
1 onion, coarsely chopped
1 clove garlic, crushed
250 g cooked shelled mussels
200 g cooked marinara mix or shelled prawns
125 g cooked calamari tubes
250 g kingklip, filleted, cubed and cooked
1 tomato, coarsely chopped
½ green sweet pepper, seeded and chopped
375 ml Cheese Sauce (page 37)
2 ml dried oregano
5 ml salt
2 ml milled black pepper

250 g puff pastry
a little milk

FILLING: Heat the oil in the skottelbraai. Sauté onion and garlic until golden, then add remaining ingredients. Simmer until just heated through — about 5 minutes. Remove from heat and divide mixture between six casserole bowls (or place in one large casserole bowl).
Roll out puff pastry. Cut six discs slightly larger than casserole bowls. Cover bowls with discs of pastry (wetting edge of bowl if necessary). Cut slits in pastry to let steam escape. Brush pastry with milk. Bake pies in pizza oven until golden.
SERVES 6

Seafood Crêpes

Although easy to make, these crêpes are distinctive enough to serve to special guests. The pancakes may be made in advance on the stove (and frozen), or cooked over the coals.

PANCAKE BATTER
375 ml cake flour
2 eggs
15 ml sunflower oil
450 ml mixed water and milk
a little sunflower oil

FILLING
600 g kabeljou or kingklip fillets
600 ml milk
60 ml butter
2 sticks celery, chopped
5 ml curry powder
45 ml cake flour
salt and milled black pepper to taste
75 ml cream
150 g shelled and cooked prawns

60 ml grated Cheddar cheese
chopped fresh parsley

PANCAKE BATTER: Whisk flour, eggs, oil and half the milk and water until smooth. Whisk in remaining liquid. Oil a small cast-iron frying pan lightly and spoon in about 30 ml batter, tipping pan to spread it. Cook for 1 minute over the coals, or until golden underneath, then flip and cook the other side. Repeat, making twelve pancakes altogether. Keep warm, covered.

FILLING: Poach fish in milk in a cast-iron pot over the coals for 10 minutes, or until easy to flake. Strain off and reserve liquid, and flake fish. Melt butter in a skottelbraai, add celery and curry powder and stir-fry for 1 minute. Stir in flour, reserved liquid and salt and pepper. Bring to boil, stirring, then simmer for 1 minute. Remove from heat and fold in cream, flaked fish and prawns.

Divide filling between crêpes. Roll up crêpes and place in a single layer in a greased shallow oven-proof dish. Sprinkle grated cheese over and cover loosely with foil. Bake in a pizza oven until bubbling — about 30 minutes. Serve at once, garnished with chopped parsley.
SERVES 6

VARIATION
Instead of the prawns, use chopped, cooked seafood of your choice.

Batter-dipped Crayfish

Use the smallest (legal) crayfish that you can find for the most succulent results. Langoustines or king prawns are equally delicious prepared this way.

6 small crayfish tails, cooked and shelled

BATTER
50 g cake flour
90 ml cornflour
pinch salt
1 egg, separated
150 ml ice water

30 ml sunflower oil
Peri-Peri Sauce (page 36) to taste

Halve the crayfish lengthways.
BATTER: Mix the flour, cornflour and salt and make a well in the centre. Whisk the egg yolk with the water and pour into the well. Draw in flour from sides of bowl and beat until smooth. Whisk egg whites until stiff and fold carefully into the batter.

Heat the oil in the skottelbraai. Dip crayfish tails in batter and fry in the hot oil until crisp and golden — about 5–7 minutes. Serve immediately with the sauce.
SERVES 6

Mussel Potjie

Add any seafood to the mussels: crayfish is tasty but expensive; white fish fillets are more economical.

10 ml sunflower oil
1 onion, sliced
2 cloves garlic, crushed
1 green pepper, seeded and sliced
1 perlemoen, cleaned, sliced and pounded or 2 tuna steaks
250–300 g calamari tubes
2 whole crayfish
24–36 mussels, cleaned
5 ml salt
5 ml chopped fresh oregano
1 bay leaf
5 ml lemon juice
30 ml tomato paste
125 ml beer or dry white wine

Heat oil in a cast-iron pot and sauté onion and garlic until transparent. Add the green pepper, perlemoen, calamari, crayfish and mussels. Stir in remaining ingredients and simmer over braai fire for about 1 hour, or until seafood is tender. Serve with Pot Bread (page 43) or brown rice.
SERVES 6

Seafood Fondue

Don't use trimmings from an oily fish for the stock.

STOCK
1 small onion, chopped
3 sprigs fresh parsley
1 kg white fish bones and trimmings
1,25 litres water
juice of ¼ lemon
5 ml salt
6 white peppercorns
400 ml tomato juice
60 ml sherry

SAUCES
Fresh Tomato Sauce (page 36)
Hot Garlic and Anchovy Sauce (page 36)
Horseradish, Dill and Caper Sauce (page 37)
Sweet-and-Sour Sauce (page 37)

SEAFOOD
18 large prawns, cleaned and deveined
assorted fish cubes, oily and white fish (such as kingklip, tuna, yellowtail, monkfish, hake)
small calamari tubes or thickly sliced rings
crab sticks, cut into 5-cm chunks

STOCK: Place onion, parsley and fish bones and trimmings in a cast-iron pot and add water, lemon juice and salt. Simmer gently, covered, for 20 minutes. Skim during cooking. Add peppercorns and simmer for a further 10 minutes. Strain and discard fish trimmings. Add tomato juice and sherry and pour half of sauce into a cast-iron fondue pot. Simmer over low coals. Reserve remainder at side of braai fire to top up fondue as needed.
TO SERVE: Place sauces in serving bowls. Skewer seafood and fish on fondue forks and cook in simmering stock. Dip in sauce.
SERVES 6

Seafood Pizza

One of the problems with making home-made pizzas is that most people shy away from yeast baking. The easy-to-make dough used for this pizza effectively removes that objection; and the topping is both the easiest in the world to prepare and the tastiest to eat!

DOUGH
500 ml cake flour
15 ml baking powder
2 ml salt
60 ml butter or margarine
1 egg, beaten
125 ml milk

TOPPING
50 ml Fresh Tomato Sauce (page 36)
1 x 200-g can tuna or salmon, drained and broken into chunks
1 x 85-g can smoked mussels, drained
8 black or green olives
1 large ripe tomato, sliced
4 canned artichoke hearts (or 8 canned asparagus spears), drained
2 large black mushrooms, sliced
mixed grated mozzarella and Parmesan cheese to taste

DOUGH: Sift the flour, baking powder and salt together, then rub in the butter until the mixture resembles fine breadcrumbs. Mix the egg and milk and add to the flour. Mix to a soft dough and press into two pizza pans or form into two large or six smaller rounds and place on baking sheets.
TOPPING: Spread pizza bases with Fresh Tomato Sauce. Arrange seafood and vegetables on top and sprinkle with cheese.
  Bake in a pizza oven until sizzling and cheese has melted — about 10 minutes. Serve immediately.
SERVES 6

VARIATIONS
Any combination of seafood may be used, including marinara mix. Peri-peri or chilli mussels may be used instead of smoked.

Garlic-Basted Perlemoen Steaks

Don't use frozen perlemoen for this recipe — it will be tough. Fresh perlemoen prepared in this way is a gourmet's delight.

4 perlemoen, cleaned, sliced and beaten (page 6)
10 ml lemon juice
coarsely milled black peppercorns to taste
coarsely milled salt to taste
50 ml Garlic Butter Sauce (page 36)
lemon wedges

Prepare perlemoen slices (see Note below), then brush with lemon juice. Sprinkle both sides of slices with peppercorns and salt and pat into flesh with your hands. Heat Garlic Butter Sauce in a cast-iron frying pan over hot coals and fry perlemoen steaks quickly on both sides. Serve immediately with lemon wedges.
SERVES 6

NOTE
Perlemoen must be beaten well or it will be tough when cooked.

VARIATION
Alternatively, brush the perlemoen steaks with melted Garlic Butter Sauce and braai briefly on either side on the grid over moderate coals.

Marinara Stir-Fry

Use the seafood of your choice, and in whichever quantities you require. Remember, however, that if you increase the quantity of seafood, you should also increase the quantity of vegetables proportionally.

45 ml sunflower oil
1 large iceberg or cos lettuce, shredded
2 sticks celery, cut into matchsticks
1 medium carrot, cut into matchsticks
1 clove garlic, crushed
6 baby mealies
400-g packet marinara mix
10 ml soy sauce
salt and milled black pepper to taste

Heat 15 ml of the oil in a skottelbraai until smoking. Add the lettuce and stir-fry for 30 seconds. Transfer to a serving dish and keep warm. Heat the remaining 30 ml oil and stir-fry the celery, carrot, garlic and baby mealies for 2–3 minutes, adding more oil if necessary. Reduce heat, then add marinara mix and soy sauce. Stir-fry for 2–3 minutes. Season, spoon on top of lettuce and serve immediately.
SERVES 4–6

Prawns Peri-Peri

The marinade is excellent with all kinds of seafood and fish, especially steamed mussels and clams.

MARINADE
125 ml olive or sunflower oil
30 ml lemon juice
1 clove garlic, crushed
2 bay leaves
2 ml peri-peri powder
5 ml ground cloves

12–18 king prawns, cleaned

MARINADE: Mix ingredients together well.
  Pour marinade over prawns and marinate for 2 hours. Braai prawns over moderate coals for about 6 minutes, turning and basting often with the marinade. Serve immediately, accompanied by savoury rice.
SERVES 6

Braaied Crayfish

Langoustines may also be prepared in this way.

6 crayfish
90 ml melted butter
3 ml salt
3 ml milled black pepper
15 ml lemon juice mixed with 150 ml melted butter

Clean and butterfly crayfish (page 5). Brush with melted butter and place on a hinged grid. Braai over hot coals for about 10 minutes, basting often with butter. Season. Serve immediately with lemon butter.
SERVES 6

SEAFOOD • 29

Accompaniments

Included in this chapter are recipes for all the accompaniments to a braai which turn a simple outdoor meal into a feast.
The simple, delectable salad and vegetable dishes use readily available ingredients and complement fish and seafood perfectly.
To add a gourmet touch to braaied fish and seafood, for little cash or culinary effort, there are a variety of distinctive sauces.
Marinades and basting sauces make all the difference to fish that is inclined to be dry or have a gamey flavour. They can also be thickened and served as a sauce.
Flavoured butters are among the easiest of flavour enhancers to make and can be used for most kinds of fish and seafood. They can also be melted and used as basting sauces.
The scrumptious selection of breads includes those that can be made over the coals, in the pizza oven or in a kettlebraai.
As a mouth-watering treat to end a meal, the choice of desserts range from the simple to the elaborate.

Red Roman with Piquant Yoghurt Sauce (page 20), Black Mushroom with Tomato Sauce and Cheese (page 33) and Brinjals Peri-Peri (page 33); Seafood Pizza (page 29); Olive Bread (page 43); Mexican Corn Bread (page 41); Braaied Crayfish (page 29).

Salads & Vegetables

The choice of salads and vegetable dishes given here are a bit more unusual and imaginative than those usually served at a braai.

Stuffed Onions in Foil

We are all familiar with onions braaied in foil, but these stuffed onions are decidedly different. Either pack them into an oven-proof dish and cook them in the pizza oven or kettlebraai, or wrap them in foil and cook them in the coals at the edge of the braai fire.

6 large onions, par-boiled

STUFFING
15 ml chopped fresh parsley
2 ml chopped fresh thyme
pinch ground mace
4 slices bread, crusts discarded, crumbled
65 g butter or margarine, melted
65 ml finely chopped cashew, pecan or walnuts
65 ml finely chopped sultanas
salt and milled black pepper to taste
a little milk
cold butter

Remove centres of onions and chop finely.
STUFFING: Mix chopped onion centres with the herbs, spices and breadcrumbs. Stir in melted butter, then add nuts and sultanas and season to taste. Add a little milk if the mixture is too dry.

Pack stuffing into hollowed-out onions and dot each onion with butter. Cook until onions are tender, either in the pizza oven or kettlebraai, or, wrapped in foil, in the coals of the braai fire.
SERVES 6

Mozzarella, Tomato and Olive Salad

A simple, yet classic, Italian salad that can be prepared in a jiffy and complements most braaied food.

12–18 slices mozzarella cheese
3 large ripe tomatoes, thickly sliced
100 g black olives
chopped fresh tarragon, parsley or coriander

DRESSING
100 ml light olive oil
30 ml tarragon vinegar or lemon juice
5 ml salt
2 ml coarsely milled black pepper
2 ml lightly crushed mustard seeds or 1 clove garlic, crushed

Arrange the cheese and tomato slices alternately in two concentric circles on a platter. Pile olives in centre of platter and sprinkle fresh herbs over.
DRESSING: Shake all ingredients together in a screw-top jar and drizzle over the salad just before serving.
SERVES 6

Couscous Salad

Do not leave the cast-iron pot on the coals for more than a couple of minutes, as the couscous will brown too much. There should be sufficient residual heat in the cast-iron pot to steam the couscous away from direct heat.

15 ml sunflower oil
500 ml couscous
500 ml chicken stock
15 ml butter or margarine
15 ml chopped fresh mint
1 clove garlic, crushed
1 small ripe tomato, skinned and chopped
½ small green sweet pepper, seeded and chopped
½ small red chilli, seeded and chopped (optional)
125 ml sunflower seeds

Heat the sunflower oil in a flat-based cast-iron pot over moderate coals, and stir in the couscous. Brown slightly, then add the chicken stock and remove pot from the coals. Cover with lid and leave couscous to swell in the residual heat for 15 minutes. Fluff in the butter with a fork. If serving immediately while still warm, stir in remaining ingredients. To serve as a salad, first cool the couscous and then add remaining ingredients.
SERVES 6

Herbed Baby Potato Salad

An excellent potato salad, in which the dressing brings out all the flavour of the vegetables and herbs.

1 kg small new potatoes
125 ml finely chopped onion
125 ml finely chopped fresh parsley
50 ml snipped chives
10 ml chopped fresh basil
1 clove garlic, crushed
3 rashers bacon, crisply fried and crumbled

DRESSING
100 ml sunflower or olive oil
30 ml wine vinegar
5 ml salt
2 ml milled black pepper

Boil the potatoes in their jackets until just tender — about 15 minutes. Drain and peel potatoes and place in a salad bowl. Add the onion, herbs, garlic and bacon.
DRESSING: Combine all ingredients and pour over potatoes while they are still warm.
Either serve salad immediately or leave to cool before serving.
SERVES 6

Brinjals Peri-Peri

A really different way to prepare brinjals for the braai, and both inexpensive and easy to make.

6 small brinjals
salt
2 ml peri-peri or cayenne pepper, or to taste
50 ml olive oil
5 ml fresh oregano

Slice unpeeled brinjals thickly lengthways. Sprinkle slices with salt and leave to sweat for 30 minutes. Rinse under cold water and pat dry. Combine the peri-peri with the oil and oregano in a shallow dish and add the brinjal slices. Marinate for 15–30 minutes, turning once. Braai on the grid, turning once, for about 15 minutes. Brush with any left-over marinade while braaiing.
SERVES 6

Mealie Meal Polenta

The Italian basic has become a braai favourite in this country. The onion, chilli, garlic and herbs may be left out if desired. Serve the squares at room temperature once set, or fry them as described in the recipe.

15 ml olive oil
1 onion, thinly sliced
1 small chilli, seeded and thinly sliced
1 clove garlic, crushed
750 ml chicken stock
375 g yellow mealie meal
10 ml chopped fresh oregano
125 ml grated Parmesan cheese
100 g butter
2 ml salt
2 ml milled black pepper
olive oil for frying
fresh oregano

Heat the 15 ml oil in a cast-iron pot over moderate coals and sauté the onion until transparent. Add the chilli and garlic and sauté a further 2 minutes. Stir in the stock and simmer over low coals for 15 minutes, then stir in the mealie meal and cook, stirring occasionally, until thick — about 10 minutes. Add more stock or water if the mixture becomes too thick. Add oregano and cook for a further 3–5 minutes, stirring constantly, then stir in the cheese, butter, salt and pepper. Remove from the coals and pour into a rectangular dish. Smooth mixture and refrigerate until firm — for 10–15 minutes. Cut into 5-cm squares. Heat olive oil in a skottelbraai or a cast-iron pot over moderate coals. Fry the polenta until it is golden brown. Garnish with oregano leaves.
SERVES 6

Baked Mealies

Mealies are easy and delicious to cook at a braai. Peel back the husks of the mealies carefully and discard the silks. Rub softened Sage Butter or Mustard Butter (page 40) onto the kernels, fold the husks back into place and secure them with string. Braai the mealies 30 cm above glowing coals for 15 minutes, turning occasionally. Serve immediately.

Black Mushrooms with Tomato Sauce and Cheese

These mushrooms are best cooked in individual ramekins in the pizza oven, but they can also be baked in one large oven-proof dish in the kettlebraai.

6 large black mushrooms, wiped clean and stems removed
salt and milled black pepper to taste
Fresh Tomato Sauce (page 36)
grated Parmesan cheese
dried breadcrumbs
chilled butter or margarine

Place the mushrooms, stem side up, in individual ramekins and season well. Top with Tomato Sauce. Combine Parmesan cheese and dried breadcrumbs and sprinkle over Tomato Sauce. Dot with butter or margarine and bake in a very hot pizza oven until mushrooms are tender and cheese has melted — about 15 minutes.
SERVES 6

Marinated Baby Vegetables

This salad looks elegant, and keeps well in the refrigerator for up to a week.

200 g baby marrows, blanched and thickly sliced
400 g button mushrooms, stems removed
100 g baby carrots, lightly blanched
250 ml black or green olives
200 ml olive oil
juice of 1 lemon
5 ml finely chopped fresh chives
10 ml finely chopped fresh herbs of your choice
5 ml salt
5 ml milled black pepper

Combine the vegetables and olives lightly in a bowl. Mix the olive oil and lemon juice well and pour over vegetables. Sprinkle herbs over and season with salt and pepper. Toss salad lightly and chill for at least 2 hours before serving.
SERVES 6

SALADS & VEGETABLES

Sambal Selection

Perfect with Tandoori Fish (page 24) or traditional South African dishes like Smoorvis (page 20) or Fish Bobotie (page 25), these sambals can be chosen to complement the main ingredients in the dishes they accompany.

QUINCE
1 quince, peeled and grated
2 ml salt
1 small onion, grated
1 small chilli, finely chopped
30 ml sugar

ONION AND TOMATO
2 large ripe tomatoes, skinned and chopped
1 onion, chopped
1 small green pepper, seeded and chopped
2 drops Tabasco sauce
5 ml salt
2 ml milled white pepper

LOQUAT
1 kg loquats, peeled, stoned and chopped
1 onion, chopped
2 drops Tabasco sauce

GREEN APPLE
1 tart green apple, cored and chopped
2 ml salt
1 small onion, grated
1 small chilli, finely chopped
30 ml sugar

CUCUMBER
1 large cucumber, peeled and coarsely grated
30 ml vinegar
5 ml finely chopped fresh dill
5 ml salt
2 ml milled white pepper

QUINCE: Sprinkle quince with salt. Mix with other ingredients. Pack into a ramekin.
ONION AND TOMATO: Combine all ingredients and pack into a ramekin.
LOQUAT: Combine all ingredients well and pack into a ramekin.
GREEN APPLE: Sprinkle apple with salt. Mix well with other ingredients, then pack into a ramekin.
CUCUMBER: Combine all ingredients and pack into a ramekin.
SERVES 6

Apricot Onion Relish

This relish keeps very well, but it must be refrigerated. For a slightly different flavour, add finely chopped coriander leaves to taste before refrigerating.

1 kg onions, finely chopped
200-g can smooth apricot jam
200 ml wine vinegar
5 ml mild curry powder
65 ml sugar
2 ml salt

Place the onions in a dish. Mix the other ingredients together and pour over the onions. Stir to mix well, cover and refrigerate overnight. Stir once, then pack into sterilized jars and seal tightly. Refrigerate.
MAKES ABOUT 1,5 KG

Corn and Tomato Salsa

You can use halved baby mealies instead of whole-kernel corn and cherry tomatoes instead of sun-dried tomatoes.

125 ml cooked whole-kernel corn
30 ml minced and drained sun-dried tomatoes packed in oil
30 ml thinly sliced onions
30 ml finely chopped red onion
1 clove garlic, puréed with 1 ml salt
5 ml minced fresh chilli
15 ml fresh lime or lemon juice
7 ml white wine vinegar
30 ml olive oil
30–45 ml finely chopped fresh coriander leaves
salt and milled black pepper to taste

Stir all ingredients together. Serve with braaied fish.
SERVES 6

VARIATION
To make Avocado Salsa, mix together 3 skinned and chopped ripe tomatoes, 1 crushed clove garlic, 2 finely chopped spring onions, 1 chopped avocado pear sprinkled with lemon juice, and salt and pepper to taste. Spoon onto sliced cucumber and serve.

Beefeater Tomatoes with Sweetcorn

The big, fleshy tomatoes called beefeaters are the best for this simple dish, although you can use smaller ones if you wish.

6 beefeater tomatoes
salt and milled black pepper to taste

FILLING
425-g can cream-style sweetcorn
finely chopped fresh basil to taste
a little thick cream
½ chicken stock cube, crumbled
30 ml butter or margarine
finely grated Rosetta or Cheddar cheese to taste

Cut off the top of each tomato and scoop out pulp. Reserve pulp for another use, or add to the filling, if desired. Turn tomatoes upside down to drain, then season well with salt and pepper.
FILLING: Combine the sweetcorn, basil, enough cream to moisten and the stock cube. Divide mixture between tomato shells, dot each with butter and sprinkle with grated cheese.
Either pack in a dish and bake, covered, in a pizza oven or closed kettlebraai, or pack individually in foil and braai over moderate coals until cooked and cheese has melted. Serve hot.
SERVES 6

Hedgehog Potatoes

Scrub potatoes well under cold running water, then slice them deeply crosswise. Insert slices of butter — flavoured (page 40) if you wish — between the slices and sprinkle the potatoes with seasoning and grated Parmesan cheese. Wrap them in foil (shiny side inside) and bake them in pizza oven or among the braai coals for about 45 minutes. Vary flavours and seasoning according to your personal taste.

Black Mushrooms with Tomato Sauce and Cheese, Mealie Meal Polenta, Baked Mealies and Brinjals Peri-Peri (all page 33).

SAUCES

This selection of sauces offers a medley of flavours to add a special touch to most kinds of braaied fish, seafood or vegetables.

PEANUT SAUCE

Serve with kebabs or skewered fish, or vegetable crudités. Keep, covered, in the refrigerator for up to a week.

125 g chunky or smooth peanut butter
lemon juice to taste
soy sauce to taste
milled black pepper to taste
2 ml Tabasco sauce
a little natural yoghurt, if needed

Combine all ingredients well, adding yoghurt to moisten if mixture is too stiff.
SERVES 6

TARTAR SAUCE

The sauce can include capers, finely chopped black or green olives, or any other pickle you fancy. It keeps very well if refrigerated.

375 ml mayonnaise
5 ml finely chopped fresh parsley
5 ml finely chopped fresh chives or garlic chives
1 medium pickled gherkin, very finely chopped

Mix all ingredients together well.
SERVES 6

VARIATION
For instant 'make-do' tartar sauce, mix equal quantities of sandwich spread and mayonnaise.

HOT GARLIC AND ANCHOVY SAUCE

A versatile sauce that goes equally well with vegetable crudités, baked potatoes and braaied butterflied fish. If you wish, use smoked mussels or canned sardines instead of anchovies.

200 ml olive oil
4–5 cloves garlic, crushed
12 anchovies, drained and chopped
100 g butter

Place oil in a saucepan, add garlic and heat until soft but not brown. Add anchovies and cook, stirring, over low heat until anchovies dissolve, taking care not to burn garlic. Add butter and heat until melted. Serve hot with chopped green peppers, celery, carrots, cauliflower, mushrooms, fennel, artichoke hearts, turnips, spring onions, beetroot, boiled potatoes and Jerusalem artichokes. Serve lots of bread for mopping up the sauce.
SERVES 6

GARLIC BUTTER SAUCE

Serve with white fish, line fish, game fish and stronger-flavoured fish as well as all kinds of seafood.

250 g butter
4 cloves garlic, crushed
5 ml salt

Melt butter in a saucepan over low heat. Add garlic and salt, and stir to mix well. Keep warm, covered, at edge of braai fire.
SERVES 6

VARIATION
To make Lemon Garlic Butter Sauce, add 15 ml lemon juice with the garlic and salt. For Peri-Peri Sauce, add 2 ml peri-peri or Tabasco sauce.

FRESH TOMATO SAUCE

Make a day in advance and refrigerate until needed, or make over the coals at the braai.

15 ml olive oil
1 kg tomatoes, skinned, seeded and finely chopped
2 ml crumbled dried thyme
salt and milled black pepper to taste

Heat the oil over moderate heat until hot but not smoking and cook the tomatoes, thyme and seasoning, stirring, for about 10 minutes or until the tomatoes are soft and sauce thickened.
SERVES 6

Garlic Sour Cream Sauce

This is the perfect topping for baked potatoes. And nothing could be simpler to make — except, perhaps, the variation that uses onions instead of garlic. Rosemary may be used instead of tarragon, if the latter is unavailable.

250 ml sour cream
1 clove garlic, crushed, or 5 ml bottled crushed garlic
10 ml chopped fresh tarragon or 5 ml dried

Mix all ingredients together well and pack into a ramekin. Refrigerate until needed. Quantities may be doubled, if necessary.
SERVES 6

VARIATIONS
For an onion flavour, instead of garlic and tarragon, use 1 onion, minced, and a pinch of snipped chives, or use 30 ml white or brown onion soup mix.

Sauces: Sweet-and-Sour; Peanut; Horseradish, Dill and Caper; Fresh Tomato; and Tartar (all pages 36 and 37).

Sweet-and-Sour Sauce

This sauce goes well with firm-fleshed fish like tuna and yellowtail. It can also be used as a marinade or basting sauce, particularly for seafood.

30 ml vinegar
20 ml sugar
5 ml tomato sauce
10 ml cornflour
7 ml soy sauce
125 ml very finely chopped canned pineapple (reserve canning liquor)
30 ml sunflower oil
2 medium onions, very finely chopped

Combine the vinegar, sugar, tomato sauce, cornflour, soy sauce and pineapple liquor made up to 300 ml with water. Bring to boil over moderate heat and continue cooking, stirring occasionally, until thickened. Add the oil and continue to boil for 1–2 minutes. Stir in the pineapple and onions and use immediately.
SERVES 6

Horseradish, Dill and Caper Sauce

Horseradish is not often thought of as a seasoning for fish, but it goes extremely well with braaied game fish, trout and salmon trout. The sauce must be made in a double boiler on the stove.

60 ml softened butter
4 egg yolks
500 ml cream
salt and milled black pepper to taste
30 ml horseradish sauce
30 ml chopped capers
60 ml chopped fresh dill

Whisk butter, egg yolks and cream in the top of a double boiler, over simmering water. Continue whisking until thickened slightly, then fold in rest of ingredients. Serve immediately.
SERVES 6

Basic White Sauce

This sauce has a medium or coating consistency; for a thinner sauce use 15 ml butter and 30 ml flour.

250 ml milk
30 ml butter
65 ml cake flour
salt and milled white pepper to taste

Bring milk to simmering point. Melt butter in a heavy-based saucepan over low heat, then remove from heat. Add flour and stir to make a roux. Return to heat and cook for 2 minutes, stirring. Remove from heat and gradually add warm milk, stirring constantly. Return to the heat and simmer over low heat for 5 minutes, stirring often. Season with salt and pepper and serve.
SERVES 6

VARIATION
To make Cheese Sauce, mix 125 ml grated Cheddar cheese with 2 ml mustard powder and stir into hot sauce just before serving.

SAUCES • 37

MARINADES

These tasty marinades and basting sauces not only season braaied fish and seafood, but also tenderize the flesh and prevent it from drying out. They are great with kebabs.

ROSEMARY MARINADE

Use any herbs instead of rosemary. Try dill or fennel for an unusual flavour, and a little mint jelly.

65 ml white vinegar
65 ml sunflower oil
5 ml chopped fresh rosemary
salt and milled black pepper to taste
quince jelly or mint jelly to taste

Mix all ingredients well and use to marinate fish for about 2 hours for a subtle flavour. Use left-over marinade as a basting sauce for fish.
MAKES ABOUT 135 ML

SPICY HONEY MARINADE

A marvellous basic marinade which works well for fresh snoek or other strong-flavoured fish.

125 ml dry white wine
20 ml tarragon vinegar
1 clove garlic, crushed or 5 ml bottled crushed garlic
1 small piece fresh ginger, crushed
20 ml sunflower or light olive oil
45 ml honey
5 ml chopped fresh mint
salt and milled black pepper to taste

Combine all ingredients in a saucepan and bring to a simmer. Cover and set aside for 1 hour. Pour over fish and marinate for about 2 hours. Any left-over marinade may be heated, thickened with a little cornflour and served as a sauce with the braaied fish.
MAKES ABOUT 200 ML

APRICOT MARINADE

The strong flavour of apricots goes particularly well with angelfish. For a more intense flavour, use puréed fresh apricots or cooked and puréed dried apricots instead of the jam.

75 ml smooth apricot jam
30 ml brown sugar
3 cloves garlic, crushed or 2–5 ml bottled crushed garlic
15 ml cornflour
2 bay leaves
30 ml red wine vinegar
15 ml salt
5 ml milled black pepper

Combine all ingredients in a saucepan and simmer over low heat, stirring occasionally, until slightly thickened. Use to marinate fish for about 2 hours, then use as a basting sauce for fish.
MAKES ABOUT 170 ML

LEMON AND GARLIC MARINADE

This is the perfect marinade for fish or seafood kebabs. To enhance the citrus flavour, add 1–2 fresh lemon leaves, crushed. For a subtle flavour shift, use orange juice instead of lemon juice.

15 ml sunflower oil
100 ml lemon juice
½ onion, finely chopped
1 clove garlic, crushed or 5 ml bottled crushed garlic
3 sprigs fresh rosemary
salt and milled black pepper to taste
mustard powder to taste

Mix all ingredients well. Marinate kebabs for at least 2 hours, turning occasionally. Use left-over marinade as a basting sauce.
MAKES ABOUT 125 ML

Olive oil, rosemary vinegar, Spicy Honey Marinade (page 38), Rosemary Marinade (page 38), Tomato Basting Sauce (this page) and Lemon and Garlic Marinade (page 38).

Lemon Garlic Basting Sauce

For a stronger flavour, add 5–10 ml finely grated lemon peel to the sauce.

15 ml lemon juice
2 cloves garlic, crushed or 2 ml bottled crushed garlic
75 ml sunflower oil
125 ml dry white wine
5 ml brown sugar
salt and milled black pepper to taste

Combine all ingredients well and use as a basting sauce.
MAKES ABOUT 225 ML

Tomato Basting Sauce

The perfect basting sauce for line fish.

30 ml tomato paste
30 ml snipped chives
1 clove garlic, crushed or 1 ml bottled crushed garlic
1 ml ground coriander
1 ml cayenne pepper
salt and milled black pepper to taste
125 ml wine vinegar
10 ml lemon juice

Mix all ingredients together well and use as a basting sauce for line fish.
MAKES ABOUT 200 ML

VARIATIONS
Instead of the snipped chives and coriander, try 30 ml basil or marjoram.

Herbed Basting Sauce

This is a basic basting sauce. Halve the quantities of herbs if using dried.

125 ml sunflower or olive oil
1 clove garlic, crushed or 1 ml bottled crushed garlic
5 ml very finely chopped fresh rosemary
5 ml very finely chopped fresh marjoram or oregano
5 ml very finely chopped fresh parsley
5 ml very finely chopped fresh chives or garlic chives
salt and milled black pepper to taste

Mix all ingredients together very well and use as a basting sauce for braaied fish.
MAKES ABOUT 150 ML

MARINADES • 39

BUTTERS

The interesting variations for flavoured butters given here are suitable accompaniments for most kinds of fish and seafood, or even vegetables.

SAGE BUTTER (BASIC METHOD)

Use with Baked Mealies (page 33) or as a topping for line fish.

125 ml softened butter
30 ml finely chopped fresh sage
salt and milled black pepper to taste

Mix all ingredients well and form into a roll. Wrap in wax paper. Chill until firm.
MAKES ABOUT 150 ML (SERVES 6)

VARIATIONS
Tomato Butter: Use 10 ml finely chopped, skinned and seeded tomato and 2 ml finely chopped fresh basil instead of sage.

Mustard Butter: Instead of 30 ml sage, use 10 ml mustard powder and 5 ml prepared whole-grain mustard.

Anchovy Butter: Instead of 30 ml sage, use 5 anchovy fillets, drained and very finely chopped and 5 ml lemon juice.

Garlic Butter: Use 1 clove of garlic, crushed or 5 ml bottled crushed garlic and 10 ml very finely chopped fresh parsley instead of 30 ml sage.

Herb Butter: Use 30 ml finely chopped fresh herbs of your choice instead of sage.

Seafood Butter: Instead of 30 ml sage, use 30 ml very finely chopped cooked shrimps or prawns, 15 ml finely chopped parsley and 5 ml lemon juice.

Paprika Butter: Instead of 30 ml sage, use 5 ml paprika and 5 ml minced onion.

Sage Butter, Mustard Butter, Herb Butter, Paprika Butter, Anchovy Butter and Tomato Butter (all this page).

BREADS

Freshly-baked, wholesome bread is a popular accompaniment at a braai and this selection offers a wide variety of recipes to choose from.

MEXICAN CORN BREAD

Although the correct cornmeal to make this bread is not available in this country, a mixture of mealie meal and cake flour is an acceptable substitute.

180 g yellow mealie meal
60 g cake flour
15 ml sugar, or to taste
10 ml baking powder
5 ml bicarbonate of soda
5 ml salt
250 ml grated sharp Cheddar cheese
3 fresh chillies, seeded and finely chopped (optional)
2 jumbo eggs
375 ml buttermilk or natural yoghurt
45 ml butter

Heat a flat-based cast-iron pot over the braai fire or in a pizza oven. Sift mealie meal, flour, sugar, baking powder, bicarbonate of soda and salt together, then stir in the cheese and chillies, if using, and toss well. Whisk the eggs and buttermilk together. Melt the butter in the pot and whisk into the buttermilk mixture. Working quickly, add buttermilk mixture to mealie meal and flour mixture and stir until well combined. Pour into the heated cast-iron pot, cover and bake in the ash of the braai fire, heaping coals up around it, for 45 minutes to 1 hour, and piling some coals on the lid for the last 15 minutes. Alternatively, bake, uncovered, in a pizza oven or the kettlebraai (with the lid on) for 25–30 minutes. The bread is baked when it recedes from the sides of the pot and the top is slightly browned. Serve warm.

SERVES 6–8

GRIDDLE CAKES

Quick to make and marvellous to eat, these griddle cakes are the perfect accompaniment to all kinds of fish and seafood braais. They are particularly good served with Braaied Harders (page 15) and kebabs, or as a sweet snack, served hot with honey and butter, or with a selection of jams, preserves or grated cheese.

240 g cake flour
30 ml baking powder
10 ml salt
30 ml sugar
1 jumbo egg
500 ml milk
30 ml sunflower oil

Sift together the flour, baking powder, salt and stir in sugar. Beat the egg, milk and oil together and mix into the flour mixture. Heat and grease a griddle over moderate coals. Drop spoonfuls of mixture onto the griddle. Cook over the coals until golden, first on one side and then on the other. Repeat until all the batter has been used.

SERVES 6

OATCAKES

Scottish oatcakes were traditionally cooked on the griddle (or girdle) over the coals, so they will really be quite at home cooked over the braai fire. They can also be baked in a conventional oven at 190 °C for about 20 minutes, or in a pizza oven. If you want to make sweet oatcakes, add 125 ml brown sugar instead of the salt.

200 g butter or margarine
375 ml pinhead oatmeal
375 ml wholewheat flour
2 ml salt
a little milk

Cream the butter until smooth. Mix the oatmeal, flour and salt together and work gradually into the creamed butter to make a stiff dough. Moisten with milk, if necessary. Roll out to about 10 mm thick on a floured board and cut out rounds with a biscuit cutter. Grease a griddle or a flat-based cast-iron pot and place some of the oatcakes on it. Cook over moderate coals for about 5 minutes, or until golden underneath, then flip and cook the other side. Eat hot, buttered, or allow to cool first.

SERVES 6–8

Pot Bread

This is the classic 'bush' bread, which is just as popular for an urban braai. Bake the basic bread recipe given here, or try any of the variations that follow.

1 kg white bread flour
10-g packet instant dry yeast
10 ml sugar
10 ml salt
625 ml warm water
15 ml butter

Combine the flour, yeast, sugar and salt in a large bowl. Add the warm water and mix to form a stiff dough. Knead manually or in a food processor until elastic — about 5 minutes. Knead the butter into the dough and leave to prove, covered, until doubled in size. Knock down and place in a well-greased flat-based cast-iron pot. Leave to rise again. Bake, covered, directly on low coals for 45–50 minutes, or until golden. Pile some coals on top of the lid as well. Alternatively, bake, uncovered, in the kettlebraai (with the lid closed).
SERVES 8–10

VARIATIONS
Wholewheat Pot Bread: Use a mixture of 500 g wholewheat flour and 500 g white bread flour.

Askoek: Make dough as for Pot Bread and bake the bread directly on the coals or in the ashes.

Roosterkoek: Make dough as for Pot Bread, roll dough out lightly and cut into cakes. Leave to rise, then braai on a grid over the coals, turning once. Serve with butter and jam.

Bread on a Tile: Follow the basic Pot Bread recipe, but place the dough on a flat, unglazed terracotta tile after it has risen. Sprinkle with coarse salt and sprigs of rosemary and bake in a hot pizza oven or in a kettlebraai with the lid closed for 40–45 minutes.

Bread on a Tile (this page), Pot Bread (this page), Mexican Corn Bread (page 41), Olive Bread (this page), Beer Bread (this page) and Potato Scones (this page).

Olive Bread: Slice 250 ml drained black olives from the pips and knead into the dough after kneading in the butter. Bake as for Bread on a Tile.

Stick Bread: Mould small quantities of the Pot Bread dough into spirals around clean sticks (not oleander) or thick skewers, covering the ends of the sticks too. Cook over low coals for 15–20 minutes, turning often. (Bread is done when it will slip easily off the stick.) Slip bread off the stick and serve with butter in the hollow.

Peasant Bread

Because it does not contain baking powder or yeast, this bread does not rise very much, but its coarse texture and excellent flavour make it an exceptional accompaniment to braais and potjies. The bread can also be baked in the same way as Bread on a Tile (this page). It goes particularly well with Tandoori Fish (page 24) and Prawns Peri-Peri (page 29).

720 g white bread flour
60 ml olive or sunflower oil
salt to taste
enough milk to mix

Mix all ingredients together to form a stiff dough. Knead thoroughly to spread the oil through the dough, then form into a ball. Pinch off into six pieces and flatten each to about 5 mm thick. Bake on both sides on a grid over moderate coals, or on a griddle, and serve hot with butter.
SERVES 6

VARIATIONS
Garlic Peasant Bread: Sprinkle 2 cloves garlic, crushed, or 10 ml dried crushed garlic and a little coarse salt over each round before baking in a pizza oven or kettlebraai, lid closed. Do not turn over.

Herbed Peasant Bread: Add 125 ml grated Parmesan cheese to the dry ingredients and sprinkle 15 ml mixed dried herbs and a little coarse salt over each round. Bake as for Garlic Peasant Bread.

Olive Peasant Bread: Stone and chop about 250 ml black olives and press into bread rounds, sprinkle each with coarse salt and bake as for Garlic Peasant Bread.

Beer Bread

This has to be the easiest loaf of all to make, as it is simply a mix-and-bake recipe. It is also versatile — add grated cheese, or minced onion, or whatever savoury flavouring you fancy to the dough before baking.

500-g packet self-raising flour, either white or wholewheat
340 ml beer
5 ml salt

Mix all ingredients together and spoon into a greased loaf pan. Bake in the pizza oven or the kettlebraai (with the lid closed) until the loaf recedes from the sides of the pan and the loaf sounds hollow when tapped — about 45 minutes. Or bake at 180 °C in an oven for 1 hour, or until receding from the sides of the pan. Brush with melted butter or oil when baked to prevent the crust from hardening. Serve with butter.
SERVES 4–6

Potato Scones

The secret of making light potato scones is to prepare them while the potatoes are still hot and cook them over the coals at once.

500 g skinned and cooked potatoes
salt to taste
125 g cake flour
a little sunflower oil

Mash the potatoes well with the salt while they are still hot. Knead the mashed potato to a dough with the flour and press out to required thickness. Cut into triangles. Brush a griddle with oil and place scones on it. Bake scones on both sides over the coals until they are golden and serve immediately, with butter.
SERVES 6

BREADS • 43

DESSERTS

Dessert is a favourite with everyone. This tempting collection offers an assortment of sweet treats to prepare beforehand or at the last minute.

APPLE AND BERRY CRUMBLE

A new way with an old favourite, which can be varied according to what fresh fruit is available.

FILLING
750 g canned pie apples
250 g fresh youngberries or blueberries, or 410-g can, drained
grated peel of 1 lemon
30 ml brown sugar (optional)
5 ml ground cinnamon

TOPPING
75 ml butter or margarine
110 g sugar
110 g cake flour

FILLING: Combine all ingredients and place in a lightly greased pie dish.
TOPPING: Cream the butter or margarine and sugar in a bowl, then work in the flour until the mixture resembles fine breadcrumbs. Sprinkle over the filling.
  Bake at 180 °C in a conventional or pizza oven until lightly browned — about 45 minutes. Serve the dessert hot with cream or custard.
SERVES 6

VARIATIONS
Dried Fruit Crumble: *Use stewed dried peaches, apricots or mixed fruits instead of apples and youngberries.*

Rhubarb Crumble: *Use cleaned and sliced rhubarb instead of apples.*

Plum Crumble: *Use stewed plums and chopped preserved ginger instead of the apples and berries.*

PUMPKIN FRITTERS

The all-time South African favourite is perfect for serving as the finishing touch to a special braai. As a variation, use Hubbard squash or butternut instead of pumpkin.

750 ml cooked mashed pumpkin
2 eggs, separated
5 ml salt
240 g self-raising flour
sunflower oil for frying
ground cinnamon mixed with brown sugar

Beat the pumpkin, egg yolks and salt together in a bowl. Sift the flour and mix into the pumpkin mixture. Whisk the egg whites until stiff peaks form and fold into the pumpkin mixture. Brush a cast-iron frying pan, flat-based cast-iron pot or a griddle with oil. Drop tablespoonfuls of pumpkin mixture onto the pan or griddle and fry for 2 minutes on either side, or until golden. Serve fritters hot, sprinkled with cinnamon sugar.
SERVES 6–8

BRANDIED FRUIT TART

An easy-to-make fruit tart that is served with a tipsy brandy sauce. Rum may be used instead of brandy, if you wish, and the canned fruit may be varied to taste.

240 g self-raising flour
375 ml sugar
2 large eggs
10 ml bicarbonate of soda
425-g can fruit cocktail, youngberries or cherries

BRANDY SAUCE
250 ml milk
315 ml sugar
45 ml butter
15–30 ml brandy

Mix the flour, sugar, eggs and bicarbonate of soda together in a large bowl. Fold in the canned fruit and juice and mix carefully. Pour into two greased pie dishes and bake at 180 °C for 20–25 minutes, or until lightly golden and springy to the touch.
BRANDY SAUCE: Just before the end of baking time, combine the sauce ingredients in a saucepan and bring to the boil. Boil for 3 minutes.
  Remove the tarts from the oven and pour the hot brandy sauce over immediately. Serve with custard.
SERVES 8–10

Frozen Nectarine Mousse

If you are making this delectable fruity mousse for a special occasion, freeze it for at least 8 hours and turn out onto a pool of strawberry purée to serve.

375 g nectarines, pitted and chopped
10 ml fresh lemon juice
250 ml sugar
125 ml water
4 large eggs
250 ml chilled thick cream
sprigs of fresh mint
fresh strawberries, halved

Combine the nectarines, lemon juice, 65 ml of the sugar and the water in a saucepan and simmer, stirring occasionally, for 10–15 minutes, or until reduced to about 65 ml and nectarines are very soft. Purée and cool. Whisk eggs with remaining sugar in the top of a double boiler over simmering water until four times the volume. Cool. Whisk cream until it just holds stiff peaks and fold into egg mixture. Fold nectarine purée in carefully. Pour into a spring-form pan and freeze until set. Release spring-form sides and leave mousse on base. Garnish with mint and strawberries.
SERVES 6–8

VARIATIONS
Any other soft fruit may be used instead of nectarines — apricots, strawberries and other berry fruits (depending on availability) are particularly suitable.

White Chocolate Mousse

This is really rich, so a little goes a long way. Serve with a fruit purée or a fruit sauce. If you have the time, the mousse can be poured into a large dish and set in the refrigerator.

150 g white chocolate, broken into pieces
4 large eggs, separated
375 ml thick cream
15 ml castor sugar
15 ml brandy
Flake chocolate bar

Melt white chocolate in a bowl over simmering water, then allow to cool to room temperature. Whisk egg whites until stiff. Whip cream and sugar together lightly. Beat egg yolks very lightly and fold into melted chocolate, then stir in brandy until smooth. Fold a little of the whisked egg whites into the chocolate mixture, then fold the chocolate mixture into the rest of the egg whites. Whip the cream and sugar again until stiff, then fold into chocolate mixture. Pour mousse into six small ramekins. Freeze until firm. Decorate with crumbled Flake.
SERVES 6

Walnut and Fig Fridge Tart

This is an easy and versatile fridge tart, which can be varied by choosing different canned fruits and nuts.

450 g green fig preserve in syrup
50 ml custard powder
25 ml sugar
45 ml butter or margarine
125 ml coarsely chopped walnuts
175 ml condensed milk
200-g packet Tennis or Marie biscuits
sweetened whipped cream

Drain the figs and chop all but 1 coarsely. Slice reserved fig lengthways and set aside until needed. Make the syrup up to 500 ml with water and mix it with the custard powder and sugar. Bring to the boil over low heat, stirring. Continue to cook for 1 minute, still stirring, then remove from the heat and stir in the butter or margarine. Cool slightly. Add chopped figs, half the walnuts and the condensed milk to the custard mixture and mix well. Layer half the Tennis biscuits in a buttered rectangular glass dish and pour half the custard mixture over. Layer remaining biscuits on top and spread remaining custard mixture over. Chill until set, then decorate with remaining walnuts and sliced fig. Serve with whipped cream.
SERVES 6

VARIATIONS
Instead of fig preserve and walnuts, use a can of youngberries or black cherries, drained, and chopped almonds. Or use a can of apricots, drained, and chopped pecan nuts.

QUICK AND EASY DESSERTS

Tropical Melons: This is the perfect fruity dessert. Turn three halved and seeded gallia melons upside down in a sieve to drain, then place in dessert bowls. Fill with tropical fruit (such as sliced ripe mangoes, halved litchis and sliced banana, which has been sprinkled with lemon juice to prevent it from browning) and sprinkle with kirsch or Grand Marnier or cassis. If you wish, you can top lightly with cinnamon sugar (use castor sugar). Set aside for 1–2 hours before serving. Alternatively, top thickly with cinnamon sugar and place under a grill for a few seconds to melt sugar, then serve immediately.

Fruit Kebabs: The sauce adds something special to this fruit dessert. Thread fruit of your choice (like canned black cherries, fresh strawberries, cubes of pineapple and pear, slices of banana, grapes and canned litchis) onto long metal skewers. Make a basting and dipping sauce by heating 375 ml honey, 100 ml water and 30 ml brandy together in a saucepan. Add 100 ml evaporated milk, if you wish. Keep the sauce warm next to the braai fire. Brush the kebabs with the sauce, then braai them, turning often, for 5–7 minutes. Dip kebabs in sauce to serve.

Granadilla Cream: This dessert is a wonderful combination of tart and sweet flavours. Heat the pulp of 12 fresh granadillas with 45 ml sugar over low heat until sugar dissolves, then remove from heat. Heat 500 ml thick cream in another saucepan to boiling point, then remove from heat and stir into granadilla mixture. Spoon into six dessert glasses. Chill until set.

Barbados Cream: This is a simple version of crème brulée. Whip 375 ml thick cream until thick but not stiff. Carefully fold in 375 ml natural yoghurt. If you wish, you can fold in chopped fresh fruit at this stage (or pour the cream over the fruit). Spoon into six dessert glasses and sprinkle brown sugar thickly over the top. Refrigerate until the dessert is set and the sugar has formed a thick crust — about 6 hours.

Apricot Sorbet

Plums work very well for this sorbet, and so do nectarines and berry fruits.

100 g sugar
200 ml water
juice of 1 lemon
500 g very ripe apricots, stoned
15–30 ml orange essence (optional)

Simmer sugar and water until sugar dissolves, then add lemon juice and bring to boil, stirring occasionally. Syrup should thicken slightly. Cool slightly, then purée with apricots and orange essence, if using, until smooth. Pour into ice-cube trays, cover with cling-wrap and freeze until hard. Process or blend to a very soft cream. Return to freezer, covered with cling-wrap, until ready to serve.
SERVES 6

Baked Pears

This is a variation on the classic pears in red wine, which can be baked in a conventional oven or in a pizza oven.

6 large, firm cooking pears
250 g castor sugar
250 ml dry Marsala, sherry or port
1 cinnamon stick
a few drops vanilla essence
150 ml water

Stand unpeeled pears in a large oven-proof dish. Combine remaining ingredients and pour over and around the pears. Bake, uncovered, in a conventional oven at 150 °C for 1½–2 hours, or in a moderate pizza oven. Baste from time to time with the juices, and check that pears are tender before removing from the oven. Serve hot or cold, with cream.
SERVES 6

Quick Vanilla Ice Cream

This ice cream is easy to make and easy on the palate. You don't have to make a custard first and there is no repeated beating and freezing.

5 egg whites
750 ml cream
397-g can condensed milk
pinch salt
5 ml vanilla essence

HOT CHOCOLATE SAUCE
75 ml butter or margarine
60 g cocoa powder
45 ml sugar
45 ml golden syrup or treacle
5 ml vanilla essence
50 ml water

Whisk the egg whites until stiff peaks form. In another bowl, beat the cream until thick, and fold in the condensed milk. Add salt and vanilla essence, then fold egg whites in carefully. Freeze until firm.
CHOCOLATE SAUCE: Blend all ingredients well in a saucepan and heat gently, stirring, until butter melts. Heat until hot, then pour over ice cream to serve.
SERVES 6

Berries with Liqueur Cream

This is a quick and easy dessert to make when berries are in season. Use an appropriate liqueur for the berries you choose.

500 ml berries of your choice (such as youngberries, strawberries, blueberries, gooseberries)
castor sugar
Cointreau, cassis or other liqueur
250 ml thick cream
citrus peel curls

Wash and pick over berries. Divide between six dessert glasses. Sprinkle with castor sugar and a little liqueur. Cover with cling-wrap and chill for at least an hour. Just before serving, whip the cream until doubled in volume, fold in a little castor sugar and liqueur to taste and divide between dessert glasses. Decorate with citrus peel curls and serve.
SERVES 6

Pumpkin Fritters (page 44), Walnut and Fig Fridge Tart (page 45), Barbados Cream (page 45), Granadilla Cream (page 45) and Baked Pears (this page).

INDEX

abalone *see* perlemoen
alikreukel 4, 6
    Chilli Grilled Mussels (var.) 13
Anchovy Butter (var.) 40
angelfish 4
    Braaied Garlic Angelfish 23
    Fish Thermidor 18
    Kabeljou Provençale (var.) 23
Apple and Berry Crumble 44
Apricot Marinade 38
Apricot Onion Relish 34
Apricot Sorbet 46
Askoek (var.) 43
Avocado Salsa (var.) 34

Baked Mealies 33
Baked Pears 46
Barbados Cream 45
Basic White Sauce 37
Beefeater Tomatoes with
    Sweetcorn 34
Beer Bread 43
Berries with Liqueur Cream 46
Black Mushrooms with Tomato
    Sauce and Cheese 33
Blackened Fish 25
Bobotie, Fish 25
Bouillabaisse over the Coals 10
braai equipment 6–7
braai utensils 7
Brandied Fruit Tart 44
Bread on a Tile (var.) 43
Breyani, Fish 25
Brinjals Peri-Peri 33
Burgers on the Braai, Fish 25
butterfish 4

calamari 4, 5, 6
    Calamari Medley 12
    Whole Sardines with Mustard
        Sauce (var.) 13
Cape salmon *see* geelbek
carp 4
    Rainbow Trout with Almond
        Butter (var.) 18
Cheese Sauce (var.) 37
Corn and Tomato Salsa 34
Couscous Salad 32
crayfish 4, 5, 5–6
    Batter-Dipped Crayfish 28
    Braaied Crayfish 29
    Crayfish, Mussel and Sausage
        Gumbo 11
Crêpes, Seafood 28
Crostini 15
Crusty Tomato Soup with Mixed
    Seafood 10
Cucumber Sambal *see* Sambal
    Selection

Dried Fruit Crumble (var.) 44

elf 4, 5
    Rainbow Trout with Almond
        Butter (var.) 18

fire, preparing the 7
Fondue, Seafood 28
Fresh Tomato Sauce 36
Frikkadel Kebabs 13

Frozen Nectarine Mousse 45
Fruit Kebabs 45

galjoen 4, 5
    Butterflied Snoek (var.) 21
game fish:
    Game Fish Steaks with Olives
        and Tomatoes 21
    Tuna with Peppercorn Crust
        (var.) 20
Garlic Butter (var.) 40
Garlic Butter Sauce 36
Garlic Peasant Bread (var.) 43
Garlic Sour Cream Sauce 37
geelbek 4
    Kabeljou Provençale (var.) 23
    Red Roman with Piquant
        Yoghurt Sauce (var.) 20
    Whole Stuffed Geelbek in Foil 18
    Wine-Baked Geelbek 21
Granadilla Cream 45
Green Apple Sambal *see* Sambal
    Selection
Griddle Cakes 41
grunter 4
gurnard 4

hake 4
    Baby Kabeljou with Tomato and
        Rosemary Butter (var.) 20
    Fish Thermidor 18
    Red Roman with Piquant
        Yoghurt Sauce (var.) 20
    Sole Kiev Parcels (var.) 24
    Spicy Fish Fritters 24
    Tandoori Fish 24
    Whole Stuffed Geelbek in foil
        (var.) 18
harders 4, 5
    Braaied Harders 15
    Whole Sardines with Mustard
        Sauce (var.) 13
Hedgehog Potatoes 34
Herb Butter (var.) 40
Herbed Baby Potato Salad 33
Herbed Basting Sauce 39
Herbed Peasant Bread (var.) 43
Horseradish, Dill and Caper
    Sauce 37
Hot Garlic and Anchovy Sauce 36
hottentot 4

John Brown 4
John Dory 4

kabeljou 4
    Baby Kabeljou with Tomato and
        Rosemary Butter 20
    Blackened Fish 25
    Kabeljou Provençale 23
    Tandoori Fish 24
kingklip 4
    Kabeljou Provençale (var.) 23
    Red Roman with Piquant
        Yoghurt Sauce (var.) 20
    Tandoori Fish 24
    Whole Stuffed Geelbek in foil
        (var.) 18
langoustines 4, 5
    Batter-Dipped Crayfish (var.) 28
    Braaied Crayfish (var.) 29
leervis 4 (*see also* game fish)
    Tuna with Peppercorn Crust
        (var.) 20

Lemon and Garlic Marinade 38
Lemon Garlic Basting Sauce 39
Lemon Garlic Butter Sauce (var.) 36
line fish:
    Line Fish in Banana Leaves 20
    Line Fish in Newspaper 20
    Whole Stuffed Geelbek (var.) 18
Loquat Sambal *see* Sambal
    Selection

maasbanker 4, 5
mackerel 4, 5
marinara mix 5
    Marinara Stir-Fry 29
Marinated Baby Vegetables 33
marlin: Game Fish Steaks with
    Olives and Tomatoes 21
Mealie Meal Polenta 33
Mealie Meal Seafood Fritters 27
Mexican Corn Bread 41
Mozzarella, Tomato and Olive
    Salad 32
musselcracker 4
mussels 4, 6
    Chilli Grilled Mussels 13
    Mussel Potjie 28
Mustard Butter (var.) 40

Oatcakes 41
Olive and Anchovy Crostini *see*
    Crostini
Olive Bread (var.) 43
Olive Peasant Bread (var.) 43
Onion and Tomato Sambal *see*
    Sambal Selection
Onion Sour Cream Sauce (var.) 37
oysters 4, 6
    Chilli Grilled Mussels (var.) 13

Paprika Butter (var.) 40
Peanut Sauce 36
Peasant Bread 43
Peri-Peri Sauce (var.) 40
periwinkles *see* winkles
perlemoen 4, 6
    Garlic-Basted Perlemoen
        Steaks 29
Pies, Seafood 27
Pilaff, Seafood 27
Pizza, Seafood 29
Plum Crumble (var.) 44
Pot Bread 43
Potato Scones 43
prawns 4, 5
    Batter-Dipped Crayfish (var.) 28
    Prawns Peri-Peri 29
Pumpkin Fritters 44

Quick Vanilla Ice Cream 46
Quince Sambal *see* Sambal
    Selection

rainbow trout: Rainbow Trout with
    Almond Butter 18
river trout: Salmon Trout Parcels
    (var.) 21
red roman 4
    Red Roman with Piquant
        Yoghurt Sauce 20
Rhubarb Crumble (var.) 44
Roosterkoek (var.) 43
Rosemary Marinade 38

Sage Butter 40
salmon trout 4

Rainbow Trout with Almond
    Butter (var.) 18
Salmon Trout Parcels 21
Smoked Salmon Trout with
    Melba Toast 13
Sambal Selection 34
sardines: Whole Sardines with
    Mustard Sauce 13
Seafood Butter (var.) 40
shad *see* elf
shrimps 4, 5
silverfish 4
skate wings 4
    Skate Wings with Blue
        Cheese 23
snoek 4, 5
    Butterflied Snoek 21
    Curried Snoek Soup 10
    Kabeljou Provençale (var.) 23
    Salt Snoek Kedgeree with
        Brown Rice 24
    Smoorvis 20
sole 4
    Sole Kiev Parcels 24
Spicy Crumbed Fish Bites 21
Spicy Fish Fritters 24
Spicy Honey Marinade 38
springers: Rainbow Trout with
    Almond Butter (var.) 18
steenbras 4
Stick Bread (var.) 43
Stuffed Onions in Foil 32
stumpnose 4
Sweet-and-Sour Sauce 37
Sweet Peppers with Anchovy
    Dressing 15
swordfish 4 (*see also* game fish)
    Game Fish Steaks with Olives
        and Tomatoes 21

Tandoori Fish 24
Tartar Sauce 36
Tomato, Basil and Mozzarella
    Crostini *see* Crostini
Tomato and Onion Crostini *see*
    Crostini
Tomato Basting Sauce 39
Tomato Butter (var.) 40
Tropical Melons 45
trout 4
tuna 4, 5
    Game Fish Steaks with Olives
        and Tomatoes 21
    Kabeljou Provençale (var.) 23
    Marinated Tuna, Carpaccio
        Style 12
    Tuna with Peppercorn Crust 20
    Tuna Noodle Bake 25
tunny: Tuna with Peppercorn
    Crust (var.) 20

Walnut and Fig Fridge Tart 45
White Chocolate Mousse 45
Wholewheat Pot Bread (var.) 43
winkles 4, 6
    Chilli Grilled Mussels (var.) 13

yellowtail 4, 5
    Blackened Fish 25
    Kabeljou Provençale (var.) 23
    Medallions of Yellowtail with
        Mushrooms 12
    Red Roman with Piquant
        Yoghurt Sauce (var.) 20
    Tandoori Fish 24